ALSO BY JAMES D. TABOR

*Paul's Ascent to Paradise: The Apostolic Message and Mission
of Paul in the Light of His Mystical Experiences*

*The Book of Genesis: A New Translation
from the Transparent English Bible*

Paul and Jesus: How the Apostle Transformed Christianity

*The Jesus Discovery: The New Archaeological Find That Reveals
the Birth of Christianity* (with Simcha Jacobovici)

Restoring Abrahamic Faith

*The Jesus Dynasty: The Hidden History of Jesus, His
Royal Family, and the Birth of Christianity*

*Why Waco? Cults and the Battle for Religious Freedom
in America* (with Eugene V. Gallagher)

*A Noble Death: Suicide & Martyrdom Among Christians
and Jews in Antiquity* (with Arthur J. Droge)

*Things Unutterable: Paul's Ascent to Paradise in its Greco-
Roman, Judaic, and Early Christian Contexts*

The Lost Mary

THE LOST MARY

Rediscovering the Mother of Jesus

James D. Tabor

Alfred A. Knopf
New York
2025

A BORZOI BOOK
FIRST HARDCOVER EDITION
PUBLISHED BY ALFRED A. KNOPF 2025

Published by Alfred A. Knopf, a division of Penguin Random House LLC, 1745 Broadway, New York, NY 10019.

Knopf, Borzoi Books, and the colophon are registered trademarks of Penguin Random House LLC.

Library of Congress Cataloging-in-Publication Data
Names: Tabor, James D., [date] author.
Title: The lost Mary : rediscovering the mother of Jesus / James D. Tabor.
Description: New York : Alfred A. Knopf, 2025. |
Includes bibliographical references and index. |
Identifiers: LCCN 2024035300 (print) | LCCN 2024035301 (ebook) |
ISBN 9781101947845 (hardcover) | ISBN 9781101947852 (ebook)
Subjects: LCSH: Mary, Blessed Virgin, Saint—History of doctrines. |
Mary, Blessed Virgin, Saint—Devotion to—History.
Classification: LCC BT610 .T2367 2025 (print) |
LCC BT610 (ebook) | DDC 232.91—dc23/eng/20241029
LC record available at https://lccn.loc.gov/2024035300
LC ebook record available at https://lccn.loc.gov/2024035301

penguinrandomhouse.com | aaknopf.com

Printed in the United States of America

1st Printing

The authorized representative in the EU for product safety and compliance is Penguin Random House Ireland, Morrison Chambers, 32 Nassau Street, Dublin D02 YH68, Ireland, https://eu-contact.penguin.ie.

TO ALL THOSE WHO
REMEMBER HER WELL

AVE MARIA

Ave Maria!
You were not spared
one pang of flesh, or mortal tear;
So rough the paths your feet have shared,
So great the bitter burden of your fear.
Your heart has bled with every beat.
In dust you laid your weary head,
the hopeless vigil of defeat was yours
and flinty stone for bread
Ave Maria!

                —Rachel Field, 1940

CONTENTS

Timeline of Major Events and Figures

167–164 BC	Revolt of the Maccabees against Syrian ruler Antiochus IV
63 BC	Roman general Pompey's conquest of Judea and Galilee
44 BC	Julius Caesar murdered; civil war between Mark Antony and Octavian
31 BC–AD 14	Rule of Octavian as Augustus, first emperor of Rome
37–4 BC	Rule of Herod the Great, king of the Jews
19 BC	Possible birth of Mary, mother of Jesus
6–4 BC	Likely birth years of John the Baptizer, Jesus, and Paul
4 BC	Death of Herod the Great; Jewish revolts in Galilee and Judea
4 BC	Year of the three Messiahs: Judas Hezekiah, Simon, Athrongaeus
4 BC–AD 6	Rule of Archelaus, son of Herod, over Judea
4 BC–AD 39	Rule of Herod Antipas, son of Herod, over Galilee and Perea
4 BC–AD 34	Rule of Philip the Tetrarch, son of Herod, over eastern territories
AD 6	Revolt of Judas the Galilean following removal of Archelaus
AD 14–37	Rule of Tiberius, second emperor of Rome
AD 26–36	Rule of Pontius Pilate, Roman prefect over Judea

AD 26   Preaching of John the Baptizer and the baptism of Jesus

AD 29   John the Baptizer beheaded by Herod Antipas

AD 30   Crucifixion of Jesus

AD 36   Death of the Roman archer Pantera on the Rhine River at age sixty-two

AD 37–41   Rule of Caligula, third emperor of Rome

AD 41–54   Rule of Claudius, fourth emperor of Rome

AD 54–68   Rule of Nero, fifth emperor of Rome

AD 50s   Career and preaching of Paul

AD 62   Death of James the brother of Jesus

AD 60s   Possible death of Mary

AD 64–65   Traditional dates of the death of Peter

AD 66–68   Traditional dates of the death of Paul

AD 66–73   First Jewish revolt; Roman destruction of Jerusalem in AD 70

AD 68   Death of Nero and the end of Julio-Claudian dynasty

AD 68–69   Generals Galba, Otho, and Vitellius rival to become emperor

AD 69–79   General Vespasian becomes the sixth emperor of Rome

AD 73   Fall of Masada, final Jewish holdout

AD 79–81   Rule of Titus, son of Vespasian, seventh emperor of Rome

AD 81–96   Rule of Domitian, son of Vespasian, eighth emperor of Rome

AD 96–98   Rule of Nerva, ninth emperor of Rome

AD 98–117   Rule of Trajan, tenth emperor of Rome

AD 106   Crucifixion of Simeon, successor to James, brother of Jesus

AD 117–138   Rule of Hadrian, eleventh emperor of Rome

AD 132–135   Second Jewish revolt, led by Jewish messiah Bar Kochba

Palestine
in the Time of Jesus

◘ Herodian Fortress

Sidon

ITURAEA

▲ Mt. Hermon

PHOENICIA

Tyre

Caesarea Philippi

Raphana

Gischala

BATANAEA

GALILEE

Capernaum ● Bethsaida

Cana ● Magdala ● Sea of Galilee

Mediterranean Sea

Sepphoris ● Tiberius ● Hippos

Dion

Yarmuk

Nazareth ● Mt. Tabor ▲

Abila

Gadara

Nain

Caesarea

Scythopolis

Irbid

Wadi el-Yabis (Brook Cherith)

Sâlim ● Pella

Aenon

DECAPOLIS

SAMARIA

Amathus ◘

Gerasa

Mt. Gerizim ▲

Jabbok

Sebaste ●

Jordan

Alexandrium ◘

Joppa

PEREA

Philadelphia

Jericho

Jerusalem ● Bethany

◘ Cyprus

Bethlehem ●

Qumran ◘

Hyrcania ◘

Herodium ◘

Callirrhoe ●

JUDEA

Machaerus ◘

Gaza ●

Hebron

Dead Sea

Arnon

Masada ◘

IDUMEA

Malatha ◘

0   10   20 miles

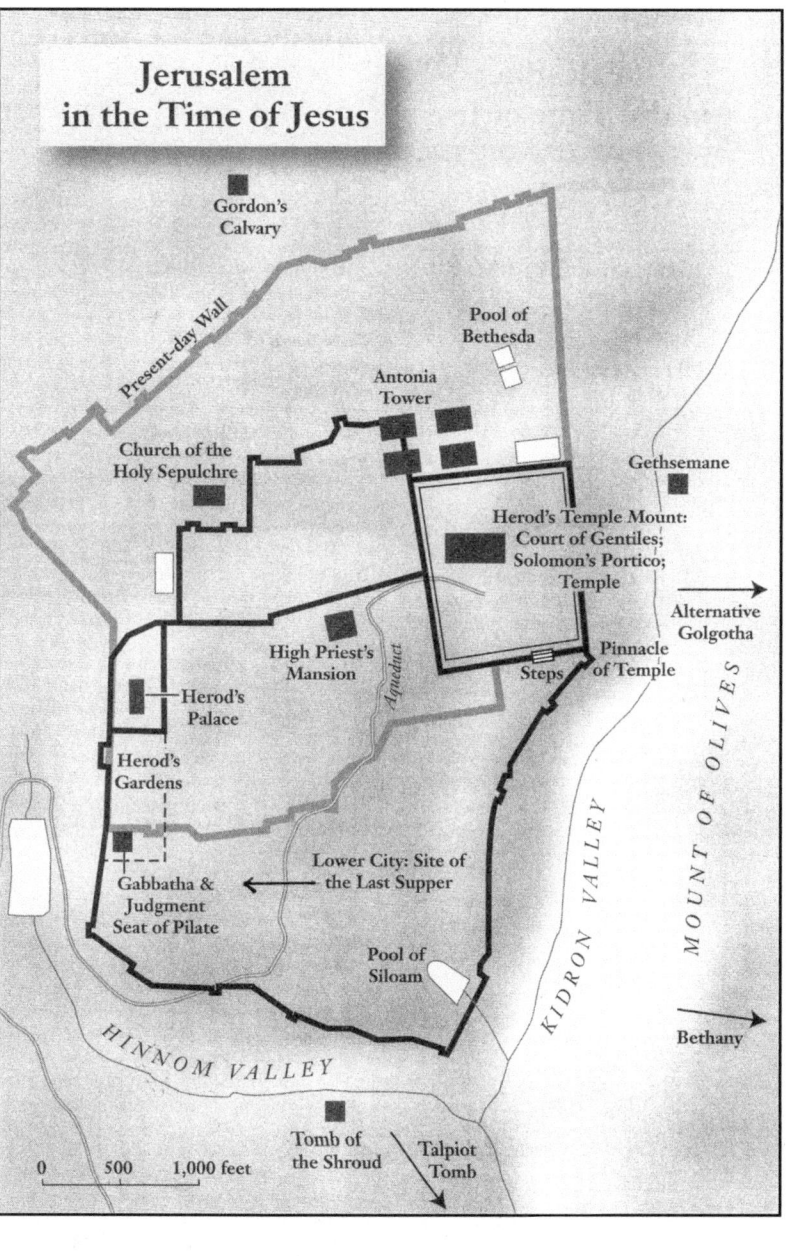

Jerusalem
in the Time of Jesus

Gordon's
Calvary

Present-day Wall

Pool of
Bethesda

Antonia
Tower

Church of the
Holy Sepulchre

Gethsemane

Herod's Temple Mount:
Court of Gentiles;
Solomon's Portico;
Temple

High Priest's
Mansion

Aqueduct

Alternative
Golgotha

Pinnacle
of Temple

Steps

Herod's
Palace

Herod's
Gardens

Lower City: Site of
the Last Supper

Gabbatha &
Judgment
Seat of Pilate

Pool of
Siloam

KIDRON VALLEY

MOUNT OF OLIVES

Bethany

HINNOM VALLEY

0   500   1,000 feet

Tomb of
the Shroud

Talpiot
Tomb

THE LOST MARY

Chapter One

FINDING THE LOST MARY

Who are my mother and my brothers and my sisters?
—Jesus

Jesus's mother, Mary, is the best-known, least-known woman in history. Recognized and revered by countless millions, at the same time she is almost wholly forgotten. I am thinking here of the historical Mary, the *real* Mary, a remarkable woman in her own time who has largely been lost to us through the thick fog of later tradition and theology.

I have spent the past two decades investigating this remarkable paradox. Towering over the ancient city of Jerusalem, just north of the Old City walls, is the Vatican's Notre Dame of Jerusalem Center. "Notre Dame" means "Our Lady" in French, referring of course to the Virgin Mary. Pope Francis stayed there on his historic visit to the Holy Land in 2014. The main building has two elaborate towers with a taller center pedestal, atop which sits a statue of a young Mary holding up her child, Jesus. She is visible from anywhere in the area, overlooking the Old City that faces the Mount of Olives to the east. I often ask my students, newly arrived in Jerusalem, "Why is there a statue of that Jewish girl, holding her Jewish baby, on top of the Roman Catholic Notre Dame Center?"

3

It takes them a moment to get the irony. Who thinks of Mary as Jewish? For most of us she is the quintessential image of a pious Catholic, very much a nun or sister in clothing and demeanor. And that seems to be our indelible cultural image of Mary, reinforced by statues, paintings, and films. Hail Mary, Mother of God, Queen of Heaven.

Mary is the most "erased" woman in history. I believe this transformation was deliberate, and as a result, finding the "real" Mary is no easy task. I am a historian of ancient Mediterranean religions, with a focus on ancient Judaism and early Christianity. I have written books on Jesus and Paul, but by far my search for Mary has been the great challenge of my career. This book is the result. I hope it will inform, surprise, and inspire readers to remember Mary as she was in her own time and place—the creative, revolutionary Jewish Matriarch of the early Christian faith.

Mary and Jesus atop the Notre Dame of Jerusalem Center

That Mary is the most notable of all women who have ever lived is indisputable. Helen of Troy, Cleopatra, Joan of Arc, and Queen Elizabeth fade into comparative obscurity next to Mary. Mary's entry in *Wikipedia* runs thirty pages, more than that of any other woman. The great museums of Western culture, from the National Gallery of Art in Washington, DC, to the Prada in Madrid or the Louvre in Paris, feature more representations of Mary than of any other person, whether paintings, drawings, frescoes, or sculptures, not to mention the innumerable holy cards, pictures, and images in countless homes, shops, public spaces, and churches. I should add that Mary is surely the most famous woman in Jewish history as well, even though, given her makeover by the Catholic Church, that fact is largely unrecognized by Jews as well as by Christians—and certainly not within our global culture.

Two and a half billion Christians plus a billion and a half Muslims—nearly half the world's population—honor her memory. Millions of Roman Catholic and Orthodox Christians hail her with the direct invocation of the Rosary: "Holy Mary, Mother of God, pray for us sinners now and at the hour of our death." Although Protestants don't pray to Mary, they remember her as the Holy and Blessed Virgin, God's chosen "vessel" to bring Jesus, the divine Son of God, into the world.

Mary, or Maryam in Arabic, is the only woman named in the Qur'an, and she has a substantial sura, or chapter, devoted to her story. The Qur'an lists Mary among the prophets; she is addressed as a "messenger" and receives more attention than the half-dozen or so other women mentioned but not named. Muslims believe she is the virgin mother of Jesus, "who guarded her private part," as God breathed into her some of his Spirit, generating her pregnancy (21:91).

And yet if we ask about the *Jewish* woman behind the images, icons, portraits, and dogmas—the real Mary, in her own time and place—little has survived, whether in popular imagination or in theological formulations.

People remember Mary as the young virgin mother of Jesus in the Christmas story who then suddenly reappears at Jesus's crucifixion. What is missing here is Mary's *entire life*.

Where did she grow up? Do we know anything about her father and mother—or any siblings, aunts, uncles, cousins in her extended family? Why do we suddenly find her pregnant and living in Nazareth in our earliest account—was that her hometown (Luke 1:26–31)? Our first account of Jesus as an adult is when he is nearly thirty years old—so what about Mary during those "missing" thirty years? There is evidence she might have lost her husband, Joseph, and ended up a widow during that period. If she had other children, do we know anything about them—how many, their names, any traditions about them? How was the family supported? Can we say anything about her daily life—as a Jewish woman of her time? Did she or his family ever travel with Jesus when he was out preaching after he went public at age thirty? Would she have encouraged him in his aspirations? Was she worried about the dangers that could result in making any kind of messianic claims or his proclamation that the "kingdom of God" was at hand, as he joined the John the Baptizer? According to the Hebrew prophets this meant a total upturn of society—politically, socially, religiously, and culturally.

And perhaps most important, when we hear the voice of Jesus—"Do good even to those who wrong you," "Don't judge by outward appearances," or "Become a servant in order to be great"—are we not hearing the voice of Mary, like any good mother, imparting to her children the principles of life and behavior from an earliest age? This book lays out the case that Jesus did not suddenly invent himself the day he was baptized by John the Baptizer and went public. He had thirty years of growing up in a large family, working in the building trades, and filling in as the eldest son in supporting Mary and assisting her in guiding the family. And so much more. Mary was not just a vessel who brought Jesus into the world; she was a proud Jewish woman with a *life* of years of devoted motherhood and guidance.

Our New Testament evidence, by some measures, could be considered sparse. She appears only a dozen or so times in our New Testament Gospels and once in the book of Acts. This rather strange omission seems hardly by chance. There is evidence that it was based on theology rather than history, and there is a good argument to be made that the downplaying of the importance of the "earthly" family of Jesus—beyond his birth—was intentional. Paul visited Jerusalem several times in the forties and fifties AD, and he mentions women often by name in his letters—but never Mary. In fact, his remark that Jesus was "born of a woman" in Galatians 4:4 seems particularly odd, since in the same letter he writes of meeting "James the Lord's brother," and staying with Peter as a guest for fifteen days on one of his visits to Jerusalem (Galatians 1:18–19). The letters attributed to Peter and John, who, according to Paul, also lived in Jerusalem and shared leadership with James, are equally silent about Mary.

However, each scene in the Gospels is rich with interpretive possibilities, hidden clues strewn along an uncharted path. Taken together and put into their historical contexts, we can lift the veil on the human Mary and catch unexpected glimpses that shatter our preconceptions and assumptions.

I have been tracking these fleeting shadowy glimpses of Mary for the past twenty years. I've done sleuthing in libraries, digging at archaeological sites, and walking the hills, valleys, and pathways Mary once trod. (I have made more than seventy trips to the Holy Land over the past three decades.) In addition to carefully reexamining New Testament materials, I have pored over important Jewish sources and newly discovered texts that have surfaced just in the past hundred years. These manuscripts and textual sources are undoubtedly exciting, but some of my most enlightening discoveries about Mary have come literally from the ground—the results of recent archaeological excavations in the Holy Land, including some in which I have been involved. From the piles of books, files, and manuscripts that surround me in my office to explorations in the ancient land of Israel, my quest has uncovered surprising revelations. Often what is not said can reveal unexpected insights, and many times a seemingly minor detail can open a whole vista of new understanding.

I have taught Christian Origins for the past four decades at the University of Notre Dame, the College of William and Mary, and the University of North Carolina at Charlotte. I could not count the times over the years when I have mentioned the four brothers and three sisters of Jesus who are named in our ancient sources, only to have a student raise a hand and say, "I had no idea that Jesus even had brothers and sisters!" My guess is that many reading this book are in the same position. This confusion about Mary and her family is understandable, since the Roman Catholic Church insists these children were cousins, whereas the Eastern Orthodox maintain they were children of her much older husband, Joseph, from a previous marriage. Neither view is found in the New Testament. The truth is, Mary herself, along with her other children, has been intentionally removed from many of our sources. As a result, our culture has inherited a mythical and legendary Mary shaped by two millennia of theology and church dogma.

I present evidence that Mary is one of the forgotten founders of earliest Christianity—very much the godmother of the

Jesus movement—in contrast to the mother of God in the Christian creeds. She apparently ended up a widow sometime before Jesus reached adulthood, as the last reference we have to her husband, Joseph, in any of our sources is one text when Jesus is twelve years old (Luke 2:41–51). Several gospel texts describe Jesus as the eldest son, head of the family. As a single parent, Mary raised her eight children under Roman military occupation through one of the bloodiest and most brutal periods of Roman history.

What I call Mary's "doubly royal" status is one of the key factors in recovering our lost Mary. She was of Davidic lineage—descended from the bloodline of King David—a royal pedigree passed on to her children. Accordingly, any of her sons was a potential candidate for the messianic throne. The prophet Isaiah had predicted that before the end of the age a descendant of David, widely spoken of as the Messiah, would usher in justice and peace throughout the entire world (Isaiah 11:1–9). But what is not widely recognized is that Mary stems from a distinguished *priestly* pedigree as well. In the Western Christian tradition this has been almost wholly forgotten. Fortunately, the evidence for her priestly ancestry survives, in a half-dozen texts, primarily preserved in Eastern sources, that have been either overlooked or marginalized.

Whatever we attribute to Jesus and the remarkable movement he inspired, Mary's vital role as the matriarch of this large Jewish family was central, both before and after the death of Jesus. Few are aware that it was her second-born son, James, with Mary by his side, who took over the leadership of the movement after Jesus's execution. The succession was dynastic, based on Mary's royal and priestly lineage. And when James was brutally stoned and beaten to death in AD 62, by the Jewish high priest Annas, his aged brother Simon assumed his place of leadership, only to be crucified under the emperor Trajan.

The ways in which Mary was gradually sidelined and written out of the story in our New Testament gospels reflects the political and theological struggles that took place among later Christian theologians who were anxious to strip her of any kind of sexuality. They also presented Peter and Paul as the coleaders of the Jesus movement, effectively writing Mary's son James out of the picture. Fortunately, we have reliable sources, in both the New Testament and shortly thereafter, that preserve an alternative narrative that fully acknowledges James as the successor of Jesus and leader of his apostles and other followers.

Mary in prayer

Christian theology, very early on, molded Mary into a passive, nonsexual, apolitical woman. She was portrayed as a pious celibate, a retiring nunlike figure, largely removed from the main drama of the story. This theologically driven counternarrative began to gain ground in the generations after her lifetime and persists in our New Testament writings. The architects of this counternarrative sought to reshape the revolutionary political message that centered on the arrival of the kingdom of God on earth into one about escaping this world and finding salvation in heaven. It became important to deemphasize and even eliminate Jesus's mortal family to focus on his exalted divinity and Mary's new role as the glorified "Mother of God." A complex mix of varied interests and forces contributed to this transformation. This desire to remove Mary from the earthly human realm to the divine heavenly sphere, while marginalizing her womanhood, motherhood, and Jewishness, was central to this theological agenda.

This book is an alternative contribution to "Marian devotions," the term millions of Christian believers use to describe their faith in Mary as the Mother of God. It is an attempt to restore Mary to her fully human life as a Jewish mother of her time.

Some may feel this historical perspective diminishes Mary's holiness or is even blasphemous, given the ideas of "perpetual virginity" that developed long after her death. I think the opposite is the case. Many believing Christians are fine with studies of the historical Jesus—including understanding him as a Jew—as a way of getting us closer to who he was in his own time. Even the idea of a married Jesus has been openly discussed and considered in our post–*Da Vinci Code* world.

It is time to pursue a similar quest for Mary. Presenting the real Mary represents an important part of such devotion. Leading scholars and historians have pioneered just such a quest in recent years, stressing the vital leadership role of early Christianity's marginalized and forgotten women. The silencing of women's voices and the negation of their achievements is deeply embedded in our historical records, including within the New

Testament itself. In Mary's case, recovering her life as a Jewish woman and single widowed mother is long overdue. By righting the cultural record, we endeavor to return women—and mothers—to their rightful place in history.

In Bruce Barton's 1925 bestseller on the life of Jesus, *The Man Nobody Knows,* he tried to strip Jesus of his theological garb and present him as a man of his time. Mary is, beyond question, the Woman Nobody Knows. I believe the multiple millions who are drawn to Mary for spiritual reasons will welcome an attempt to give Mary her life back, coming to know her as she was in her own time, freed from later church dogmas, theological formulations, mythology, and legend. The excitement of this very possibility is as inspiring as it is potentially revolutionary.

Recovering the real Mary buried in the depths of history requires careful examination of all our sources, paying particular attention to the dating of surviving evidence, which turns out to be a key factor, since the erasure of Mary and her family was progressively advanced with time.

I identify the main stages of Mary's displacement, the forces at work, and the underlying motivations, the outcomes and results, not only to shed light on what happened but to set the stage for a new era, one created for our own time: the fundamental possibility that we can resurrect the Lost Mary.

I write these words in my hotel room in Jerusalem, a ten-minute walk from Mount Zion, where Mary lived out the last decades of her life. To her and to all who honor her memory I dedicate this book: *Ave Maria.*

The Sabbath Day, April 5, 2025
Christian Quarter, Old City Jerusalem

Two Thousand
Crucifixions

Behold this child is set for the fall and rising of many
in Israel . . . and a sword will pierce through your own
soul also.

—Simon the Prophet

At age fifteen, with her infant son Jesus in her arms,
Mary witnessed the horrifying mass crucifixions carried out by the Romans just outside Nazareth, as Galilee went up in flames. The scenes she saw must have sent chills,
fear, and dread through her body, knowing that her son, as a
descendant of the royal line of King David, could well face
similar dangers.

Crucifixion was not a punishment over in a day or two or
even three—death could take up to five days. The hot sun
baked the bodies, which were stripped naked, genitals exposed
to shame the victims, family, and friends. As horrible as the
physical pain, in a Jewish culture that emphasized modest dress
and forbade the uncovering of "nakedness," this affront to basic
human decency was like a stake in the eye. Eventually, death
came from dehydration, exposure, and shock. The corpses were
left on the crosses to bloat for days before being picked clean
by wild animals, insects, and carrion birds. Nonburial, a great

affront to Jewish tradition and law, was part of the horror of crucifixion, a further deterrent to revolt.

It was the summer of the year 4 BC. That previous fall, finding herself pregnant, Mary had entered a marriage arranged by her parents with Joseph, a local artisan, who is identified as a *tekton*—this Greek word is traditionally translated "carpenter" (Matthew 13:55), but it refers to a skilled craftsman or artisan, what we might today call a "builder." Joseph was not the father but nonetheless took the baby boy as his own, and they named him Jesus, which is English for the Hebrew name Yeshua or Yehoshua. The description we get in Matthew seems to indicate that Joseph allowed the locals to assume the child was his (Matthew 1:19; 13:55).

After the birth, the couple settled in the tiny village of Nazareth in the northern part of the Roman client kingdom of Herod the Great called Galilee. Mary was still nursing her baby, who was less than a year old, when the entire country, teetering on the edge of full-scale revolt, came apart. The terrifying reality Mary experienced is far removed from the usual images associated with the birth of Jesus, "away in a manger" on a "silent night." This is indeed the post-Christmas story that nobody knows, and it had a profound effect on Mary and the sons and daughters she would raise in future years.

The Gospel of Luke offers us a concise two-verse summary of this pivotal time in Mary's life: "And when they had performed everything according to the law of the Lord, they returned into Galilee to their own city, Nazareth. And the child grew and became strong, filled with wisdom; and the favor of God was upon him." (Luke 2:39–40)

Although Luke says nothing about what was going on in Mary's world at this time, this single reference is invaluable, since we can reliably put Mary, her new husband, Joseph, and her infant son, Jesus, in the village of Nazareth in Galilee a few months after Jesus's birth. Matthew's Gospel relates that Joseph had a dream just after Jesus was born in which an angel told him to take Mary and the baby to Egypt to escape the wrath of Herod the Great, where they remained for two years, until Herod died (Matthew 2:13–15, 19–23). This flatly contradicts what I take to be Luke's more historical narrative, both in chronology and in content. Matthew also tells of their settling in Nazareth as if it were a new place for them, whereas we know from Luke it was likely Joseph's village, to which they returned just after Jesus's birth. Given this time and place, there is much we can imagine about what Mary must have experienced as the chaos ensued.

Much of what we know of the history of Mary's time, from the reign of Herod the Great (37–4 BC) to the Roman destruction of Jerusalem in AD 70, comes from the first-century Jewish historian Flavius Josephus. Initially a Pharisee, Josephus, who was of Hasmonean priestly ancestry, became a commander in the Jewish revolt against Rome (AD 66–73). He was captured by Roman forces early on and Josephus predicted that the Roman general Vespasian would become emperor, which later proved true. This prophecy earned him Vespasian's favor, sparing his life. When Vespasian rose to power in AD 69, he granted Josephus Roman citizenship and a new surname, Flavius, aligning him with the ruling Flavian dynasty. Relocating to Rome, Josephus authored key historical works, including *The Jewish War*, which provides a detailed account of the Jewish revolt, and *Jewish Antiquities*, a history of the Jewish people. His writings are crucial sources for understanding Jewish history, early Christianity, and the relationship between Rome and the Jewish people in the first century AD. Without his work little of Mary's historical background that I attempt to recover would be possible. He is that important. It is against the backdrop that Josephus provides that I am able to place Mary in the thick of things and explore her life and times beyond what our Gospels provide.

In addition to historical sources such as Josephus, the past forty years have revealed major archaeological discoveries in Nazareth, nearby Sepphoris, and a dozen other towns and villages in the area that have significantly expanded our understanding of Galilee at this time.

Nazareth was four miles southeast of Sepphoris, the urban capital of Galilee, and Sepphoris was at the center of what unfolded that spring and summer of 4 BC. From the hills surrounding Nazareth, Mary would have witnessed the unspeakable horrors taking place, literally, just outside her door.

Herod the Great, the autocratic ruler of the entire Roman-controlled land of Israel, had died in March of that year, at age seventy, following his thirty-three year reign (37–4 BC). Although Herod's death was no surprise, given his age and ill health, the unrest that followed echoed all the way to the palaces of the emperor Augustus in Rome. Augustus, whose given name was Octavian, had ended the Roman civil wars by defeating his last rival, Marc Antony, at the Battle of Actium in 31 BC, leading to his consolidation of power. In 27 BC, he took the title Augustus, meaning "revered one," and styled himself princeps or "first citizen," which masked his near-absolute power while preserving a façade of the Republic. His rule ushered in the Pax Romana, a period of relative peace and stability that lasted more than two centuries, as he reformed the military, administration, and economy, establishing the foundations of the Roman Empire.

Herod had been crowned "King of the Jews" by Augustus, even though his mother was an Arabian and his father, Antipater, an Idumean who had converted to Judaism. Most of the population considered him an illegitimate king, imposed by the force of Roman rule. During his long and prosperous thirty-three-year reign, any dissent or political unrest was successfully suppressed with the backing of four of Rome's elite legions stationed just to the north at Antioch in Syria, guarding the vital eastern boundary of the empire from any threat by the Parthians, as well as protecting the lucrative trade routes from the Far East.

Three years before his death, Herod had two of his sons, Alexander and Aristobulus, murdered out of fear that they were gaining too much favor with the people. Then, just five days before his death, Herod ordered the death of his eldest son, Antipater, heir to the throne and carrying his grandfather's name. This shocking act only further agitated the instability in the country.

Herod had left several wills as he constantly shifted his favor from one son to another. The will that the emperor Augustus declared binding divided Herod's kingdom among three of his remaining sons: Archelaus, Antipas, and Philip II. The brothers were immediately at each other's throats. Archelaus and Antipas both sailed for Rome, hoping to get the exclusive favor of the emperor. Much of the populace, spurred by messianic fervor and hope, wanted to see the Romans expelled and a native Jewish king in power, anointed as Messiah from the dynastic line of King David, who had ruled a thousand years earlier. The potential power shift had never been more precarious since the Romans had first invaded the land in 63 BC, making it part of the empire. There was no way the emperor Augustus would allow an independent Jewish state on his eastern frontier.

One month after Herod's death, at the festival of Passover in April, a vast crowd gathered in Jerusalem, threatening revolt. Passover is the festival celebrating Jewish freedom and independence from foreign rule, recalling the Exodus from slavery in Egypt in the time of Moses (c. 1400–1200 BC). Those who wanted to expel the Romans with their clients the Herodian rulers seized this moment of confusion to demand an independent Jewish state.

Mary, Joseph, and their infant son, along with her siblings and her parents, Anna and Joachim, would have made their way to Jerusalem for the festival. There they would have gathered at the magnificent temple complex that Herod had begun rebuilding and expanding in 19 BC, the year of Mary's birth. Herod's intention was that Jerusalem with its temple would stand out among all the temples of the empire in its size and splendor. Passover, of all the Jewish festivals, was a family affair, with various clans, groups, and whole villages traveling together. The Gospel of Luke tells us that as a family, accompanied by their fellow villagers, Mary and Joseph went year by year "according to custom," to these pilgrim festivals as commanded in the Torah (Luke 2:41–42). This seasonal migration involved thousands of caravans of men, women, and children, with animals and provisions. The one-hundred-mile, three-day journey had established camping stops along the route through the Jordan Valley. Once in Jerusalem, the thousands of pilgrims stayed

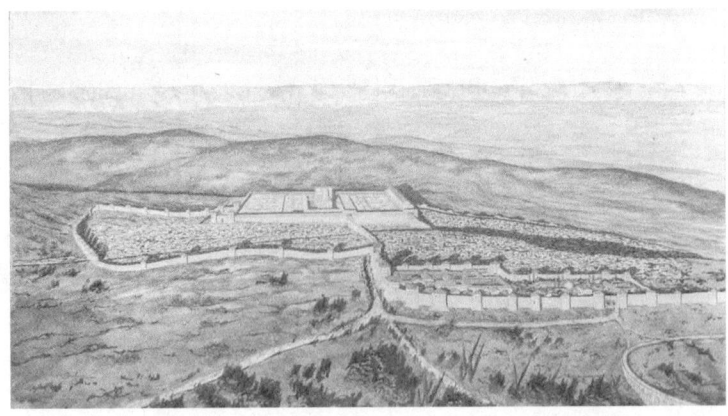

Herod's Jerusalem, with temple and royal palace

with friends, relatives, or in outdoor camps crammed around the outskirts of the walled city, crowding the nearby villages to overflowing.

Josephus reports that the enormous crowd gathered in the temple for Passover that year began to get out of control. Mary and her family were likely in the temple courts when the trouble began, since it was customary for throngs of pilgrims to gather for the beginning of the celebration, each family with a year-old lamb as a sacrifice for the Passover meal in the evening. The expanded temple courtyard measured thirty-five acres and as many as three hundred thousand people could gather there. Josephus vividly reports the chilling details of what happened next.

Archelaus, the surviving son of Herod who controlled Jerusalem, sent in a cohort of five hundred troops to quell the disturbances. He was completely unprepared for what followed. The crowd pelted them with stones, and many of his soldiers were injured or killed. Archelaus was anxious to depart for Rome, where he could make his case before Augustus that he replace his father as sole king of the Jews, rather than one of his brothers. The last thing he needed was for Jerusalem, the capital city of the entire territory, to be in full-scale revolt as he arrived in Rome. He struck back hard, calling in his entire army, including cavalry. Stones and staffs were no match for spears, arrows, and swords. Archelaus's well-armed troops brutally retaliated, killing three thousand Jews as they were in the act of slaughtering their Passover lambs, mixing their blood with that of the sacrifices. Mary, Joseph, and their baby were somewhere in the city as the crowd scattered and surely witnessed this bloodbath. One can imagine Jesus and his brothers and sisters growing up and hearing firsthand from Mary tales of these appalling events.

Thousands of others who were in sympathy with those calling for a revolt were chased out of the city to the nearby hill country. It was customary to celebrate the entire eight days of Passover in Jerusalem. This year, the newly appointed Archelaus ordered everyone to return home. The chaos and disorder that followed set the whole country on edge. The dead were from all over the country, and families had to hastily bury the mutilated bodies one by one, according to the Jewish rites of burial that entailed thirty days of mourning. The shrieks of horror and the constant wailing of groups of mourners filled every village and town. It is almost certain that Mary and her family were in the midst of it all as they made their three-day trek back to Nazareth. Doubtless they would have known some of the individuals who had been killed by Archelaus's brutal reprisal.

Generally, after a major Jewish festival, families returned home, banded together in groups according to their villages and clans, resuming their lives as farmers, tradesmen, and artisans. This year things were different. Those thousands who had scattered in hiding created massive disruption throughout the country. Revolution was in the air.

Fifty days later, at the Jewish festival of Pentecost in May of that year, virtually the entire population of the country gathered once again in Jerusalem—this time in greater numbers than usual. The tension level was at the breaking point. Once again, Mary and her extended family would have traveled to Jerusalem to observe this feast. Pentecost celebrated the giving of the Torah at Mount Sinai in the days of Moses and represented a renewal each year of God's covenant with the Jewish people. This year was far from ordinary. As throngs of pilgrims from Galilee choked the road along the Jordan Valley, many of them armed with whatever weapons or farming implements they could carry, they had one thing in mind—expelling the "foreign" sons of Herod the Great who were vying for control and, if possible, installing one of their own as ruling king. This time these warriors for Jewish independence were more organized, but still ill equipped to face the veteran troops of the Herodian family backed up by Roman soldiers stationed in Jerusalem. The Jewish forces divided themselves into three camps, north, south, and west, around Jerusalem, effectively putting the city under siege.

We don't know where Mary and her family stayed in Jerusalem that week, or how close they got to the violence brewing in the city and around the temple. We can assume they were keenly aware of what was going on. It is possible they found safe refuge with Mary's kinswoman Elizabeth, who was the mother of an infant just six months older than Jesus who became known as John the Baptizer. The Gospel of Luke reports that the year before, when Mary discovered she was pregnant with Jesus, she had fled Nazareth for the hill country of Judea, west of Jerusalem, where Elizabeth and her husband, Zechariah, a priest, lived in a tiny village known as Ein Kerem to this day (Luke 1:39).

In Jerusalem, the Roman governor Sabinus found himself surrounded by angry crowds. He was able to fortify himself in Herod's palace on the west side of the city, supported by various Herodian guards and auxiliary troops. He sent an urgent letter requesting help to Varus, the Roman legate of Syria, who commanded four Roman legions camped in Antioch to the north.

In the meantime, the fighting in Jerusalem had erupted, causing many casualties on both sides. At one point, part of the temple was set on fire. Sabinus was ultimately victorious, since the Jewish crowds were disorganized and shabbily armed; but all over the country smaller bands of Jewish rebels attacked the Herodian forces, which were in disarray. And that was just the beginning. To the east, two thousand of Herod's troops took up arms against any who might oppose them, perhaps wanting to pull off a coup independent of the Roman desire to choose the successors of Herod the Great.

It wasn't long before things exploded in the north as Mary and her family members, along with the populations of the hundreds of villages of the Upper and the Lower Galilee, returned home. Resuming a normal life was impossible, especially for Mary and her family, who lived on the outskirts of the capital city of Sepphoris, within clear sight of its city walls.

The trouble in the north was a more direct threat to Roman order than the disorganized unrest of the crowds fighting Sabinus in Jerusalem. A Jewish Galilean revolutionary named Judas, son of the rebel leader Hezekiah, who had been subdued by Herod the Great thirty years earlier, dared break into the royal armory at Sepphoris to secure weapons for his army of dedicated followers and declared himself the rightful king of Israel. The mere claim to be a "king" was an overt act of rebellion against Rome, equivalent to claiming to be the promised Jewish Messiah. This ideal native king, according to widespread anticipation based on the Hebrew prophets, would free the Jewish people from foreign occupation and establish an independent, theocratic Jewish monarchy. Many connected the appearance of such a ruler—who was expected to descend from the royal lineage of King David of old—with the "end of days" and the inauguration of the "kingdom of God" (Isaiah 11; Micah 5:2–4). We can assume that Judas, given his name and surname, claimed such Davidic lineage, since David was of the tribe of Judah and Judas's father had been named after the eighth-century king Hezekiah, who was one of the most revered of the former Davidic kings. Even though these names might be familiar to us from the Bible, their messianic, revolutionary connotations should not be missed.

The Romans had a well-practiced way of dealing with such

messianic aspirants: death by crucifixion or beheading—and sometimes both. Judas's revolt must have had the support of many inhabitants of Sepphoris, and presumably the villages such as Japha and Nazareth, clustered around the capital city. They would have had sympathy for his attempts to overthrow Roman rule and break free from Herod and his dynasty, which was considered illegitimate.

Varus marched two of his legions south to quell the revolt in Galilee, lest it spread throughout the country. Varus's short rule as the legate of Syria (6–4 BC) was characterized by cruelty and arrogance. Syria was an imperial province under the direct control of Augustus, due to its strategic importance. Varus was a friend of Augustus's, married to one of his nieces, and at the time the emperor's most trusted general. As such he had been assigned to the troubled eastern edge of the Roman Empire, where the Romans were worried about the Parthians breaking through their eastern frontier. Stability in the land of Israel was essential, and Herod the Great had delivered just that for the past forty years. Now everything was coming apart.

A Roman legion consisted of six thousand men, including elite infantry and auxiliary support personnel, so this response of upward of twelve thousand troops was decisive. Rome would tolerate no political instability or religious fanaticism. The Jews had been given various privileges, including freedom to follow their traditional religion, and exemption from any formal or official homage to the Roman deities. Rome expected peace and stability in return.

This massive influx of military forces streamed down from the north, choking the roads, scouring the countryside, and making forays into all the towns and villages of the Upper and the Lower Galilee. Their mission was to ferret out any participants or sympathizers with the cause of Jewish independence. Life was cheap and blood ran freely.

Varus's forces laid siege to Sepphoris and burnt the city to the ground, so everyone would know the cost of supporting Judas and his messianic revolt. The flames would have been visible in the night skies for miles around, especially from the hills surrounding Nazareth. Smoke filled the air as animals and people scattered. Thousands of men, women, and children were killed. Entire villages that had supported the revolt were brutally punished. Mary would have witnessed these horrific scenes firsthand, and the memories would surely have stayed with her the rest of her life.

Varus's next step was to be sure the entire country, from Galilee in the north to Jerusalem and Judea in the south, was pacified. Tens of thousands were exiled and others, mostly wives and children of the men who had fought the Romans, were sent away as slaves, for either hard labor or prostitution.

In one of the strangest twists of fate in Mary's life, one of the hundreds of Jewish families exiled following Judas's revolt was that of Saul—later known as Paul the Apostle. His parents lived in Gischala, a village just twenty-five miles north of Sepphoris. Jerome, the church father, says that they carried the infant Saul to safety, settling in Tarsus of Cilicia in Asia Minor, where they subsequently obtained their Roman citizenship. More than thirty years later, Mary's path would intersect with Paul's in Jerusalem when he went up to visit her son James, successor of Jesus, shortly after Paul had joined the Nazarene movement.

This double hammer blow of execution and exile spread terror, disorder, and resentment through the local population. Josephus tells us that the Roman legions crucified two thousand of those captured as an example to the rest of the population. As far as the eye could see, cross after cross, each with a suffering victim, lined the complex of main roads that connected the city of Sepphoris with the rest of the country. These were busy roadways, crowded with people, wagons, carts, and animals, the lifelines of trade, commerce, and travel in the thickly populated region.

Mass Roman crucifixions

Roman roads were eight feet wide, so passersby were only a few feet from the crosses that lined the edge of the roads. Such a mass crucifixion had never taken place during the sixty years that the Romans had taken control of the country.

This torturous method of execution apparently originated with the Persians. We get our English word "excruciating" from the Latin *crux*—a cross. Josephus refers to crucifixion as "that most wretched of deaths" and relates eyewitness stories of the prolonged agony it entailed. He tells of one case in which he saved the life of a friend who had been on the cross for three days:

I saw many captives crucified and recognized three of my acquaintances among them, I was cut to the heart and came and told Titus [the Roman general] with tears what I had seen. He gave orders immediately that

25

they should be taken down and receive the most careful treatment. Two of them died in the physicians' hand; the third survived. (*Life* 420–21)

Josephus was eyewitness during the Great Revolt (AD 66–70) to a scene just outside the city walls of Jerusalem that must have been quite like what Mary witnessed at age fifteen in Galilee. He reports that Titus tortured and crucified five hundred or more Jewish rebels per day:

The soldiers out of rage and hatred amused themselves by nailing their prisoners in different postures; and so great was their number, that space could not be found for the crosses nor crosses for the bodies. (*Jewish War* 5:446–451)

The Romans adopted the practice of crucifixion throughout the empire for the worst kind of offenses, especially insurrection. The clear intent was to ensure order, squelch dissent, and terrify the populace. The message was unmistakable: *Don't ever try this again.*

We know a lot about how crucifixion was carried out by the Romans against the Jews from literary accounts as well as recent archaeological discoveries in Jerusalem. In 1990, in a northern suburb, a first-century-AD Jewish tomb was discovered that contained the skeletal remains of a crucified male. His name, Yehochanan, was inscribed on his ossuary, but he is otherwise unknown to us. To the surprise of all, the rusted remains of an iron crucifixion nail was embedded in his right heel bone. Although there is a replica now on display in the Israel Museum, viewed by millions each year, the actual heel bone with the intact nail is in the anthropology lab at Tel Aviv University, where I was permitted to examine it in 2012.

Something of the brutal reality of the practice came through to me that day as I held the light piece of bone in my hand, feeling its contours through a laboratory glove.

When Yehochanan's body was taken down from the cross, the nail must have been so difficult to remove that it was hacked away from the wooden cross and left intact in the bone. Until this discovery, we were not sure just how the feet of victims were attached to the cross. We now know they were fastened to each side of an upright post with a five-inch iron nail through each heel bone—the largest bone of the foot. The idea was to secure the body, stirruplike, but not to sever any major blood vessels, lest the victim lose consciousness and quickly die.

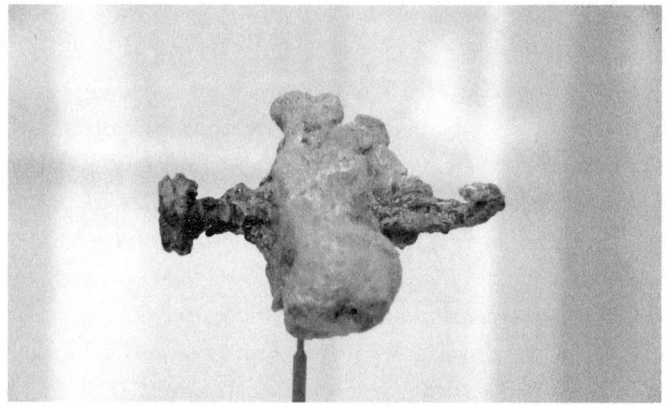

Heel bone with crucifixion nail intact,
first-century Jerusalem ossuary

With tensions already at a boil in the region, a second messianic candidate arose in Perea, east of the Jordan River. A royal slave named Simon declared himself king of the Jews, gathered followers, and burned the luxurious royal palace of Herod the Great in Jericho, near the Dead Sea. The Romans responded with full force to this blatant act. Simon and his followers were

chased back across the Jordan into Perea to the east and surrounded in a narrow ravine. Simon tried to escape on horseback but was captured and beheaded, his corpse left to rot in
the open desert. This move by Simon was significant enough
to be noted by the Roman historian Tacitus: "On Herod's
death, one Simon, without waiting for the approbation of the
emperor, *usurped the title of king.** He was punished by Quintilius Varus, then governor of Syria, and the nation, with its
liberties curtailed, was divided into three provinces under the
sons of Herod." (*Histories* 5.9) Conferring the official title of
king—which the Jews took as a messianic claim—was a right
the Romans reserved to themselves. It was this explicit claim,
thirty years later, that brought Mary face-to-face with her own
son's crucifixion, based on the royal Davidic pedigree she had
passed on to him.

Remarkably, in 2008, a stone tablet inscribed in Aramaic
was discovered in this very region of Jordan, contemporary
with these events, that refers cryptically to Simon. This text
refers to a "Messiah" whose body would be left to "rot like
dung" but who would be raised on the "third day." Fantasies,
wish fulfillment, and delusions, based on a fervent hope for the
Messiah, filled the air in conversations all over the land.

At about the same time, yet a third messianic candidate, a
shepherd named Athrongaeus, declared himself king. He had
the support of four brothers, a kind of revolutionary messianic
family not unlike Mary's, whose sons would come to prominence three decades later as the leading messianic family of
that time.

Athrongaeus and his brothers gathered a following and
began raiding throughout the country, directly attacking
Roman garrisons in Judea to the south. As a "shepherd king,"

---

* Here and throughout, italic emphasis within a quotation is mine.

he modeled his candidacy for Messiah after David of old. He and his brothers were eventually captured and executed, but only after Herod's son Archelaus had returned from Rome and been appointed ruler of Judea and Samaria by Augustus. Josephus cynically remarks that at that time, "anyone might make himself king as the head of a band of rebels."

Although none of our New Testament Gospels relate these historical events around the time of the birth of Jesus, there is a closing line in Luke's account that is apropos: "And his mother kept all these things in her heart" (Luke 2:51). This was the young Mary's world, and she and Joseph were not on the margins, but eyewitnesses to these horrific events with a front row seat. That Mary lived through this turbulent "year of the three Messiahs," as I am calling it, as a young mother with her firstborn son in her arms, paints a vivid picture for us of the dramatic forces that shaped her, her family, and the messianic movement they founded. The Gospels are focused on theology, but Mary's lived experience is our key to opening a window—or even a door—and entering her world in order to discover her again.

But there is much more. What about Mary's origins? It is common to think of the village of Nazareth, but there is evidence that she was in fact born just to the north—in Sepphoris, the urban capital of the entire country of Galilee, putting her even more in the thick of things.

Chapter Three

THE FORGOTTEN CITY
OF SEPPHORIS

A city set on a hill cannot be hidden.

—Jesus

S epphoris is a forgotten city. You won't find it in the New Testament, and until recently it was not even included on the maps of the Holy Land found in the back of many Bibles. Yet Sepphoris is a vital key for understanding Mary's origins and background.

Sepphoris, as the capital, was the hub of trade, commerce, and government for the entire region of Galilee, located in its geographic center. It was the "city set on a hill," as Jesus later put it, clearly visible for miles around to the dozens of smaller towns and villages clustered in the fertile and expansive Bet Netofa Valley.

Tradition has it that Jesus's grandparents, Joachim and Anna, parents of Mary, were from Sepphoris. If so, it was there where she would have been born and raised, not in Nazareth, where she ended up. The Gospels tell us nothing of her childhood, but it seems inevitable that legends would begin to fill this blank story. The earliest is a third-century apocryphal text, the Protoevangelium of James, which imagines the young Mary being sent by her parents to the temple in Jerusalem, at age three, to be raised by the priests there as some sort of Jewish version of a vestal virgin until age twelve—when she begins her period and would be ready for marriage. During this time she received perfect food from the hand of an angel, and various other marvels are related about her exceptional holiness as the future vessel for the birth of Jesus, the divine Son of God. An elderly Joseph is chosen by lot to be her husband, in a strictly caretaker role.

This Greek text, which circulated broadly, especially in the East, was soon translated into Latin and became the basis of most Nativity traditions down into the Middle Ages. It is first mentioned by the church father Origen in the early third century. There appears to be little in the text of historical value, as it is mainly about Mary's birth being miraculous and her virginity remaining "intact" through her childhood, and even *after* giving birth to Jesus. This doctrine of *hymen intactus* is indeed related to a traditional belief within Marian devotion. It holds that Mary remained a virgin not only before and during the conception of Jesus (*virginitas ante partum* and *virginitas in partu*) but also after His birth (*virginitas post partum*). It first appears in this apocryphal text but is defended by the major early church theologians such as Augustine and Jerome.

It might be significant, however, that the Protoevangelium of James presents Mary's father, Joachim, as "exceedingly rich," a prominent landowner with large flocks, herds, and servants. This assertion that Mary was a child of a well-to-do family might have some historical validity since this text was composed at a time when the poverty and celibacy of the Holy Family had become associated with her nunlike virtue. And yet the author presents her as coming from an influential family in the urban capital of Galilee.

There is a passing line in one of the fragmented letters of Paul where he writes of Jesus, "Though he was rich, for our sake he became poor..." (2 Corinthians 8:9). This is usually taken as a theological statement about Jesus giving up his "pre-existent" heavenly glory as the Son of God, but in context Paul is writing to urge those who have much to share with those who have little. Also, in the various early sayings of Jesus, the idea that he and his followers have "left everything," selling houses, lands, and possessions to give to the poor and support the communal life of the group, is a dominant one (Mark 10:17–31; Luke 12:32–34). This is likely the case with Mary's family as well. They are pictured in our earliest Gospel records as living in Capernaum, a fishing village on the northern shore of the Sea of Galilee, in the house of Peter's family in just such a communal arrangement (Mark 2:21, 29–31; 2:1; 3:19). And Jesus says he has nowhere he can call his own to "lay his head," with the implication that he has taken this on voluntarily, as he urges others to do the same (Luke 9:58). If Mary is presented as "high-born" in some of our sources, as we will see in subsequent chapters, there is no good reason to dismiss the idea that she comes from a wealthy, land-owning family, living in Sepphoris.

The tradition that Mary was born in nearby Sepphoris also makes geographical sense. It is first mentioned by the Italian "Piacenza Pilgrim" who visited the Holy Land in AD 570. His is one of the few detailed records about pilgrim sites of the Holy Land in late antiquity. It offers valuable descriptions of Christian sites, local customs, and the religious life in that period. Many of the places he visits and the traditions he reflects we can trace back to earlier fourth-century Byzantine times. He reports seeing the house of Mary there, associated with a cave that was said to be part of the house, as well as relics of the young virgin. There are a few earlier Byzantine remains on the grounds, including a third-century mosaic with Hebrew writing. Sometime in the twelfth century, the Crusaders built a church there dedicated to St. Anne, Mary's mother. Inside the ruins of the church is a "rock" about one meter high, left in place, rising from the floor, which usually indicates a holy spot—perhaps what was considered the remains of Mary's house. Pilgrims could see the rock behind the high altar and pray before it. I have walked its ruins as well as the later Crusader Church of St. Anne, also at the site, trying to imagine Mary as a young girl growing up there with the spectacular view of the Bet Netofa Valley to the south, crammed with surrounding villages and towns, including the suburb of Nazareth, where she and Joseph would raise their children.

Mary's possible connection to Sepphoris is what motivated me to excavate there in the 1990s. I was beginning to picture a more "urban" Mary, coming of age in a courtyard house just

Ruins of the Church of St. Anne, Sepphoris

inside the walls of this ancient city. I have also wondered, since Joachim and Anna are never mentioned in the New Testament Gospels, what sort of interactions Jesus and his brothers and sisters might have had with their grandparents as they were growing up in nearby Nazareth.

Certainly, the larger family clan would have traveled to Jerusalem together for the various Jewish festivals, and gathered for family events and celebrations—births, weddings, funerals, and Jewish observances—during all the years in which we know nothing of Jesus, his siblings, or his parents. I am thinking that few readers of the Gospels give much thought to the idea of Jesus spending time with his grandparents while he was growing up and they were living just four miles to the north in Herod Antipas's magnificent capital of Sepphoris. One can easily imagine the household excitement over the newborn baby Jesus—and all the children that followed. Both Joachim and Anna likely had great influence on this crop of sons and daughters that came along,

That we know little to nothing of Mary's family in our New Testament Gospels underlines the point that her life was of scant interest beyond the role she played in bringing Jesus into the world. Anything we know about the family, including Mary's other children, hangs on a few threads—but each of them is of enormous importance in pointing us toward recovering the lost Mary. The shared life of a large extended family, with grandparents, aunts, uncles, and cousins likely clustered in the area, allows us to constructively place Mary in a more historical light.

It seems likely that Mary had only moved to nearby Nazareth when she became engaged to Joseph the year before (Luke 1:26; 2:39). If so, it was a move from the capital city to a smaller village on the outskirts of the urban center of the region. This move would have exposed her to a markedly different social world from that of her childhood. Both were Jewish, but one was metropolitan and the other more rural and artisanal.

Even so, Nazareth was far from an isolated backwater village. It was surrounded by a range of hills adjacent to a double-walled city called Japha, a place few have heard of unless they have read Josephus, our first-century historian, who says it was the *largest village* in Galilee. I have seldom seen Japha included on maps that purport to show Galilee at the time of Jesus. Considering its size and strategic location, it is more than an insignificant omission. Josephus knew the village firsthand and had even lived there for a time (*Life* 230, 270; *Jewish War* 3.289). Nazareth was considered an extension of the larger village of Japha, a kind of hamlet within Japha's city borders. Tel Yafia, the center of this ancient urban area, is just 2,700 yards, a forty-minute walk, from the traditional location of Mary's house in the village of Nazareth. The Via Maris, the major road through Galilee, skirted the borders of Japha.

Archaeologists have identified a cultural boundary between Japha/Nazareth and Sepphoris—the former being more exclusively Jewish with the latter more multicultural and Hellenistic. Nonetheless, the whole area was prosperous and urban. But most important to our search for the real Mary is that as a young girl she would have been exposed to a diverse environment combining Jewish, Greek, and Roman cultures, high and low, in a mix that was characteristic of the multicultural region of Galilee into which she was born. And if her family was one of means, that adds significantly to how we might understand her life. Her existence in the vibrant capital city of Sepphoris brings into questions some of our traditional assumptions of Mary as an impoverished illiterate from a backwater rural village with no exposure to Greco-Roman culture. This might even account for the ways in which the Gospels portray Jesus as moving freely among the diverse economic and social strata of society, whether encountering Roman centurions or being invited to dine in wealthy homes of the time.

But back to the year of the three Messiahs. Sepphoris in flames, surrounded by the mayhem Josephus so vividly described, is a good place to pick up our story, with Mary and her family, including her parents, Anna and Joachim, in the thick of things. Total terror raged for a month or more. Anyone living in one of the dozens of surrounding villages, such as Nazareth, who was not rounded up must have cowered in fear behind closed doors or hidden in the various underground cisterns and hewn chambers beneath the ancient houses and courtyards of the Jewish villages.

This chilling reality came home to me recently when I visited Nazareth with a PBS film crew working on a documentary on the historical Jesus. Archaeologists have uncovered the remains of what appears to be a first-century-AD domestic building, most likely a courtyard house under the Sisters of Nazareth Convent, three hundred feet north of the Church of the Annunciation—where Byzantine tradition locates Mary, who was engaged but not yet married to Joseph, when the Angel Gabriel appeared to her announcing her future pregnancy (Luke 1:26–33). Nazareth is later referred to as "their town," so one might assume it was the home of Joseph (Luke 2:39). These newly uncovered remains were built up against the natural rock slope of the terrain. When the sisters acquired the place in 1881, they were told it was the site of a "great church" and had the "tomb of a saint" known as "the Just One" below. Despite some unofficial digging in the nineteenth and twentieth centuries, the site was largely forgotten until recently.

Excavations from 2006 to 2009 have identified the remains of a Byzantine church dating to the fifth century, but farther below, rock-cut structures have been dated to the period when

Mary lived there. This includes a narrow doorway, intact, resting on the original floor. Fragments of an early Roman cooking pot were found there. Even though the house is long gone, I was allowed to walk through its subterranean lower levels and could vividly imagine families hiding in the storage areas.

In 2009, in a salvage excavation in Nazareth, there was yet another significant but unexpected discovery in connection with the construction of the International Marian Center, just across the street from the Church of the Annunciation. Israeli archaeologists uncovered the partial remains of another first-century AD courtyard house dating to the time of Jesus. The Marian Center now encloses it, and it is open to visitors. The house is small and modest but likely typical of the dwellings in a village like Nazareth at that time. The exposed area consists of two rooms as well as a deep, bell-shaped cistern and a hewn-out underground pit. We wanted to film an interview in the pit, so we climbed down into the narrow cistern by ladder, barely squeezing through, until we reached the bottom. The space was hardly large enough for a single family to hide. Similar underground storage pits and cisterns are beneath the Church of the Annunciation, among ruins traditionally identified, since the Byzantine period, as Mary's house. The archaeologists believe that these underground areas were hiding places during the Great Revolt against Rome in the 60s AD, but they were no doubt used in earlier periods of crisis and insurgency as well. Sitting in that cistern, I thought of Mary in the summer of 4 BC, hiding with Jesus, Joseph, and perhaps others of his family, as the Roman legions terrorized the countryside, rounding up all suspected of supporting this Jewish revolt for independence from Rome.

No one has yet been able to identify which specific house belonged to Mary and Joseph, but multiple nearby excavations in Nazareth have uncovered several such first-century courtyard houses that give us a glimpse of what village life might have been like.

Mary not only lived through the destruction of Sepphoris but witnessed its complete rebuilding. Following the burning and sacking of the city by the Roman general Varus and his troops, Herod Antipas, the son of Herod the Great who was made the ruler of Galilee by Augustus, rebuilt Sepphoris as his showcase capital. While the city remained Jewish, it reflected the Hellenistic style of a thoroughly Romanized ruler, far surpassing any earlier splendor. Antipas was determined to match his father's massively impressive building programs, so he spared no cost or luxury for the rebuilt city.

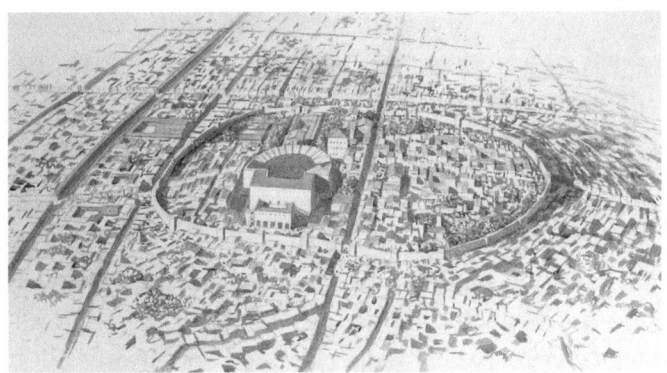

Sepphoris rebuilt in splendor by Herod Antipas

Herod Antipas, who was raised in Rome, was well known to Augustus and his imperial court. His aristocratic tastes are reflected in his various building projects, the remains of which have been excavated. Josephus, who saw the rebuilt city in its glory, calls it the "ornament of all Galilee." It was a fortified city with sturdy walls and limestone-paved streets beautifully laid out in a grid with its *cardo maximus* and *decumanus maximus*, the main intersection of a proper Greco-Roman polis, or city. The population of Sepphoris in the time of Mary is estimated at twenty thousand or more, which included dozens of surrounding villages that were its suburbs. It sported impressive public and administrative buildings, two markets, colonnaded streets, a theater, and the palace of Herod Antipas. We know the public buildings included an armory, archives, and the treasury for the city and the region. Major roads connected Sepphoris to the Via Maris, the major north-south roadway of the area, as well as west to the Mediterranean and east to the Sea of Galilee. Its water supply was perennially ensured with massive reservoirs cut into bedrock to the east of the hill upon which it was founded.

I took nine students to excavate at Sepphoris in the summer of 1996, and I continued to dig there for several seasons. We joined one of the teams led by the late Professor James Strange of the University of South Florida with a consortium of other universities and colleges. Strange began digging in 1983, and thirteen years later, his team was several years into uncovering the pillared upper levels of a first-century building and residential area about two meters below the current surface. More than two decades of excavations by several teams of archaeologists had exposed just a glimpse of this stunning city whose reconstruction Mary and her family would have witnessed.

Excavating any ancient site is always thrilling, and this was especially true in Sepphoris. One day we reached the level of a street and wall of a public municipal building that was constructed in the time of Jesus and would have been visited by villagers to pay taxes and handle various legal matters. Sepphoris, despite its splendor, was a Jewish city, and Antipas considered himself a Jew. Anyone living in Nazareth would have routinely visited the markets and municipal buildings of the city. Touching the ancient stones and brushing off ceramics and coins untouched for nearly two thousand years made that world come vividly alive. I remember reaching a burn layer from the destruction of the city in Mary's time—even after two millennia, the burnt wood still retained its smell. And the colorful mosaic floors depicting gods, goddesses, and mythical beasts, flowers, fruit, and intricate geometric patterns, when dusted off and washed, were as beautiful as they were when Mary and Jesus walked upon them in sandaled feet.

Sepphoris excavation, first-century-AD palatial building

We were digging on top of the hill where the city once stood, gazing out over the Bet Netofa Valley with the city of Nazareth plainly in view. Mary and her fellow villagers in Nazareth would have had a clear view of the burning city as they hid from the Roman soldiers. We would sit facing south, eating our breakfast in the field after an early morning of excavating that began at dawn. Some days my students and I would hike over to Nazareth for a late lunch when the day's digging was done, just to get the feel of the ancient terrain—the walk takes about forty-five minutes. We were seeking to get as close as we could to the world of Jesus and his family, both by excavating the ancient city and by exploring the area on the ground. Mary, Joseph, and their family, and other locals from the villages, knew these main roads and paths that still run between the sprawling modern city of Nazareth and the ruins of Sepphoris. The valley in between has few modern structures. The traditional ruins of Mary's house in Sepphoris are on the south side of the city, also facing Nazareth.

After the fires had gone out, the bodies were removed from the crosses, and the dead had been buried, Herod Antipas was able to reestablish an orderly rule. He reigned with a firm hand for over forty years, a time of unprecedented prosperity and peace. Based on the archaeological record, we can reliably speak of a definite boom in the economic and social life of Galilee after the devastation of the summer of 4 BC.

Of course, Joseph, along with Jesus and his brothers, had to ply some kind of trade six days a week to support the family. The rebuilding of the city of Sepphoris that stretched over the next two decades had to have been the dominant economic engine of the whole region of Galilee.

The Gospels identify Jesus as a "carpenter" and the "son of a carpenter" (Mark 6:3; Matthew 13:55). Commonly, readers take this to refer to our modern notion of carpentry, but since the Greek word translated as "carpenter" is *tekton* (τέκτων), and refers more generally to a skilled craftsman or artisan, it could just as well mean one who worked in stone. Our English word "architect" comes from the related Greek word *architekton*, or "master builder." The Gospel traditions reflect that Jesus was familiar with the building trades, and he uses images of laying solid foundations and building with stone as metaphors for the solidly built lives of his followers (Luke 6:48–49; Matthew16:18; Mark 12:10). This seems likely to reflect his profession as a skilled artisan.

If Jesus, Joseph, and his brothers worked in the building

trades at the very time that Herod Antipas was rebuilding Sepphoris, they would have made the same walk every morning to find work in the city. Mary and her daughters, up long before sunrise, would send the men of the family off for a long day working on this or that building project. Village life for Mary and her daughters would involve long hours each day centered around the whole range of domestic tasks and duties: gardening, caring for household livestock, the market, food preparation, water carrying, weaving and sewing, hygiene and medical care, and the children's care and education.

In modern Nazareth today one can visit Nazareth Village, which is an attempt to recreate, much like Jamestown and Williamsburg in the United States, what a first-century village would have been like, based on our textual and archaeological records. Everything has been constructed using ancient tools, methods, and materials—no plastic, fiberglass, wire, or manufactured metal hardware. There are houses with multigenerational expansions, a farm, synagogue, stone quarry, wells, crops, and livestock. I love visiting there, but what really comes home is how *difficult* daily life would be, since nearly 100 percent of one's time is spent in domestic chores and earning a living. Not so different from undeveloped village life all over our world today—before the advent of modern technology. From the hilltop of Nazareth Village one can see, in the distance to the north, the site where ancient Sepphoris once dominated the entire area. This view, for me at least, more than anything else connects the dots of our historically informed imagination.

In this scenario the so-called lost years of Jesus—up to age thirty, when the Gospels pick up the story—come into focus. Jesus is the oldest son of a large family in the building trades. When Joseph dies he will be expected to take over the family trade, so as he grows into manhood, Sepphoris would be on his horizon daily. This plays a major role in our quest to understand Mary as well as Jesus and his siblings. I am speculating here, of course, as Jesus's "lost years" remain lost to us. But this seems to me to be a far more likely possibility than Jesus making legendary journeys to India, Egypt, or even Britain, so popular in esoteric lore.

The attempts at armed revolution in the "year of the three Messiahs," along with the resulting chaos and violence were vivid harbingers of what was to come. The entire country was a messianic powder keg. Given her own priestly and Davidic pedigree—which we will explore in detail in the following chapters—one wonders what Mary must have thought of all that transpired. How did she view these chaotic efforts to spark a revolt, fueled by these other Davidic figures who aspired to become king of the Jews, and the carnage that resulted as the full force of Rome's legions crushed the country? Would she have condoned the violence or the methods these would-be Messiahs used to fulfill the prophetic dreams of her people? Or would she have had an equally revolutionary outlook—yet with a different vision of how it might be carried out?

Based on what we know from Josephus, much of the Jewish population was united in wanting to see an end to Roman rule, and ideally, a native Jewish king of the lineage of David. When and how this messianic revolution would come about was up for debate and speculation, but large segments of the population, based on specific prophecies in the Hebrew Bible, believed that the time was at hand.

Mary later named two of her sons Judas and Simon—names associated with these latest messianic claimants in 4 BC, as well as the more famous Maccabean brothers Judas and Simon, who led a successful revolt for independence against the Greeks a hundred and fifty years earlier, which lasted from 165 to 163 BC. This precious one-hundred-year period of Jewish freedom from foreign rule gave the priestly family of the Maccabees a kind of legendary status. It also fired the hopes and dreams of the Jewish people who believed the prophecies of the Hebrew Bible about a coming messianic era in what were called "the last days," when ordinary history would be brought to a close and the kingdom of God would fill the earth (Isaiah 2:2–4; 11:1–9). It was not so much that the Maccabees, and the priestly dynasty they formed, fulfilled those prophecies in any full and complete way, but rather that they heralded what could be possible in terms of independence from foreign rule.

"Maccabee" means "hammer," and the dynasty stemming from this family is called Hasmonean, after an ancestor, Asmoneus. Maccabean coins were popular in Mary's day, far more than the Roman "coins of the realm," and their names were as familiar as Washington, Jefferson, and Franklin are to Americans. Mary named one of her daughters Salome, after the Hasmonean mother queen Salome Alexandra, who ruled the country from 76 to 67 BC and was married, successively, to both sons of John Hyrcanus, the son of Simon the Maccabee. The names were common, but for good reason, as the Hasmonean priestly family was so revered. Of more significance, Mary herself, as we will see, was related to this priestly Hasmonean family. The name Jesus in Hebrew is Joshua—the name of Moses's successor, who conquered the land of Israel in ancient times and set up an independent Jewish state, expelling and defeating his enemies. The popularity of these names, especially in Galilee, a hotbed of revolt and messianic expectations, stemmed from their revolutionary connotations. Since these names were so popular, with half the Jewish women of the time named either Salome or Mary, some have argued that their significance is moot when it comes to Mary or her children. That ignores a simple point: the reasons such names achieved widespread use in the first place. The common denominator between Mary, Salome, Judas, and Simon, is that they are all Hebrew names favored by the Hasmoneans. As a result, their popularity is reflective of political and national sympathies among the populace in Mary's time. Mary did not choose Greek names like Alexander, Dositheus, Bernice, or Julia, or even the Hebrew names Menachem, Eleazar, Joanna, or Martha—all of which were quite popular as well. By choosing those names for her sons and daughters she was identifying with the messianic hope that God would bring about the redemption for his people as promised by the prophets.

As the matriarch of a family that could claim both royal Davidic and priestly Hasmonean lineage, Mary surely felt solidarity with the hopes and dreams of her people, but with a decidedly different view of how the messianic revolution would come about. She raised her children, including her most famous son, to appreciate that the horrifying scenes of carnage she lived through when he was not even a year old would never bring about the kingdom for which everyone longed. This unique approach to "revolution" is central to Jesus's teachings, and since his brother James reflected similar views, it was clearly a core family value.

The two images are in striking contrast: the capital city of Sepphoris in flames with Roman legions in full battle gear imposing mass crucifixions and sending thousands into exile or slavery; and the massive economic renewal spurred by Herod Antipas's rebuilding efforts that would have drawn in the populations of surrounding villages like a magnet.

No one could have known that Mary's infant son represented a more significant challenge to the stability of this troubled eastern frontier of the Roman empire than any of these revolt leaders and their followers. The threat was a different one but had everything to do with the burning issue of royal legitimacy: who in the eyes of the populace might rightly become "king of the Jews"? And this is where Mary and her family played a critical role that has gone missing from the New Testament Gospels—namely, the revolutionary political implications of this twofold royal lineage.

Chapter Four

GAME OF THRONES

You know that those who are supposed to rule over
the Gentiles lord it over them and their great men
exercise authority over them

—Jesus

Mary's birth fell right in the middle of the reign of
Herod the Great (37–4 BC), when the Jewish
population was caught up in the imminent apocalyptic expectation that the Davidic Messiah was soon to be
revealed. This is what the Hebrew prophets, Isaiah, Jeremiah,
Micah, Daniel, and others, had predicted centuries ago. Daniel
even provided a timetable for these promises that many believed
fell precisely during Mary's lifetime.

Mary's genealogical record put her generation as the seventi-
eth from Adam, expected widely to be the last before the Messiah appeared (Luke 3:23–38). As Jesus expressed it, speaking
of his own time, "This generation shall not pass away until
all these things are fulfilled" (Mark 13:30). In context, "all
these things" refers to the coming of the kingdom of God and
the judgment of the world, an apocalyptic worldview in which
all the mysteries of the prophets would be revealed. Mark,

considered by most scholars to be our earliest Gospel, opens with Jesus declaring, "The time is fulfilled: the kingdom of God is at hand; repent, and believe in the good news!" (Mark 1:15). This proclamation of an imminent messianic fulfillment was called the "good news" (or "gospel") of the kingdom of God (Luke 4:43; 8:1; 16:16).

Given the apocalyptic perspective that permeated the Jesus movement, we can be sure that Mary and her children grew up knowing the implications of their royal Davidic pedigree and its potential for playing a significant role in events. She represented not only an alternative type of revolution more potent than all Caesar's legions, but also a direct threat to Herod's fervent ambition to be accepted by the populace as a legitimate king of the Jews, founder of a new royal dynasty.

A single burning issue dominated the Roman-controlled Jewish homeland during this time: the life-or-death controversy over who could rightfully be declared king of the Jews. This ancient "game of thrones" was played out through wars, revolts, palace intrigue, betrayal, murder, and multiple assassinations. Three of Mary's sons would be murdered because of it—Jesus by crucifixion, James by stoning, and finally the aged Simon also by crucifixion—and John the Baptizer, her nephew, would be beheaded.

As a result of this controversy, Roman legions flooded the country, fleets of ships were launched, and hundreds of thousands of Jews died or were enslaved or exiled. According to our first-century eyewitness the Jewish historian Josephus, the main motivation for the Jews revolting against Rome in AD 66, was the contention over who might rightfully claim the throne as king of the Jews. The Roman legions reduced both the city of Jerusalem and the holy temple to rubble and ashes in the summer of AD 70. A final handful of 960 Jewish men, women, and children held off the tenth Roman legion at the fortress of

Masada overlooking the Dead Sea until the spring of AD 73, finally ending their lives by suicide rather than surrendering.

For much of the Jewish population, two straightforward, back-to-back commandments in the Torah of Moses established the ground rules for this game of thrones: "One from among your brothers you shall set as king over you. You may not put a foreigner over you, who is not your brother" (Deuteronomy 17:15). This meant that no foreigner would ever have the blessing of God as ruler of the Jewish people in the land of Israel. Coupled with these two Torah commandments was an unambiguous prophecy of Isaiah regarding the ideal future of Jerusalem itself: "Arise! Arise! Put on strength, O Zion! Put on your beautiful garments, O Jerusalem, the holy city; for the uncircumcised and the unclean shall never enter you again" (Isaiah 52:1).

These texts from the Jewish scriptures, along with many other biblical prophecies, predicted the coming of two messiahs— a king of the lineage of David, with a righteous priestly messiah at his side. Together they would usher in a reign of justice and peace across the earth.

I often ask my students as we begin a class on the history of early Christianity, "Who was the first Messiah?" At first, they are a bit taken aback, wanting to answer "Jesus," while being concerned that I must have something else in mind to spring on them. After all, in our culture, the word "Christ," which is the Greek word for "Messiah," seems to function as Jesus's last name! Few realize that in both Hebrew and Greek the noun "messiah" comes from the verb "to anoint." The meaning is still preserved in our term "christen," which means to anoint with the water of baptism as a way of bestowing on an infant its given name. We also speak of christening a ship for a maiden voyage—but with a bottle of champagne. In biblical times both the high priest and the king were anointed with oil in a ceremony designating them as "anointed ones"—i.e., "messi-ahs," set apart for their special roles. It was very much like our presidential inauguration ceremony with one hand on the Bible repeating the oath of office rather than an anointing with oil. Or think of the climactic pronouncement at a wedding follow-ing the exchange of vows: "I now pronounce you husband and wife." Academics call this sort of ritual "performative," in that the words and actions effect real change. One minute you're an ordinary individual, the next you're president, married, or in this case—a messiah!

Saul, the first king of Israel, was so anointed by the prophet Samuel in the tenth century BC: "Then Samuel took a vial of oil and poured it on his head, and kissed him, and said, 'Has not the LORD anointed you to be ruler over his peo-ple Israel?'" (I Samuel 10:1). His successor, David, was also anointed with oil by Samuel in a private ceremony witnessed by his father, mother, and brothers: "Then Samuel took the horn of oil, and anointed him in the midst of his brothers; and the Spirit of the LORD came mightily upon David from that day forward" (I Samuel 16:13). Therefore, both Saul and David, as the first kings of Israel, are "messiahs" or "christs" (in Greek), but they are not the first. The very first messiah was Aaron, the brother of Moses, of the tribe of Levi. The Davidic kings came along hundreds of years later.

The book of Exodus describes the formula for a mixture of olive oil, perfumes, and spices to be used exclusively by the prophets for anointing the priests and future kings of Israel (Exodus 31:22–33). Anyone else was forbidden to make this formula or use it for any other purpose. I suppose one could call it messiah oil. Moses, as the prophet of his day, poured it over Aaron's head, anointing him as high priest of Israel (Leviti-cus 8:12–13; Deuteronomy 34:10). Aaron is subsequently the "anointed" priest, which literally means the "messiah priest"

(Leviticus 4:3, 5, 16). Throughout the history of Israel, only the male descendants of Aaron could serve in this exalted role and had to be anointed with oil in an induction ceremony. That is why genealogical records were so critical.

The reason this matter is so confusing today is that Christians, Jews, and Muslims alike began to use the designation *the Messiah*—as in the one and only—to refer to the coming ideal king of the lineage of David. He is often called the "Branch of David," which literally means a "shoot" from David's line: "Behold, the days are coming, says the LORD, when I will raise up for David a righteous Branch, and he shall reign as king and deal wisely, and shall execute justice and righteousness in the land" (Jeremiah 23:5). What has been overlooked is that the Hebrew prophets also speak of the arrival of a *second* messiah—an anointed priest of the direct lineage of Moses's brother, Aaron. This priestly messiah serves alongside the Davidic king as a spiritual advisor. The sixth-century-BC prophet Zechariah is the most explicit about this. He speaks of the arrival of *"two sons of fresh oil"*—a king and a priest—who will stand before the Lord of the whole earth (Zechariah 4:12–14). *Both* are called "Branches," one a descendant of David, the other of Aaron. Later Zechariah speaks of this "Branch of David" and says that he will bear royal honor, sit and rule on his throne, "and there will be a priest by his throne and peaceful understanding shall be between them both" (Zechariah 6:12–13).

Josephus, who was an eyewitness to this fervent messianic expectation, makes two most telling observations. First, he says that what most inspired the Jews to revolt against Rome was an oracle in their sacred writings that "about this time" one from their own nation would become the ruler of the world. Second, he tells us that Herod the Great prepared the desert fortress Masada, stocking it with food and arms, in the event he and his family might have to flee for their lives if the "multitude of Jews

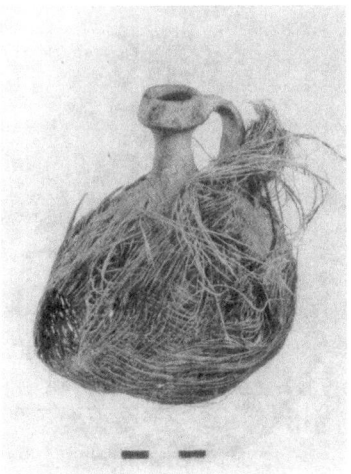

Ancient juglet of anointing oil
found in Dead Sea cave

should depose him" and put one of their own from the line of former kings on the throne." In other words, Herod feared most of all that a Jewish messianic candidate of the lineage of King David might assert himself.

Mary's historical experience was far removed from the image of singing angels, visiting wise men, and shepherds watching their flocks, sleeping in heavenly peace. In contrast, she and her family were potential players in one of the most dangerous periods of Jewish history, and her children and grandchildren came to the attention of the highest echelons of Roman rule, including the emperor himself.

To most, Herod the Great is a name in the New Testament, familiar from Christmas pageants and plays. Few are aware of the cast of world-famous characters with whom he was directly involved before and after Mary's birth. These include Julius Caesar, Cassius and Brutus, Marc Antony and Cleopatra, and Octavian, who became Augustus Caesar. Syria, Judea, and Galilee were all central to Roman interests in the area. Herod the Great cunningly managed to survive the turmoil over the civil wars between these key players that fractured Roman rule in the eastern provinces in the last decades of the first century BC.

Herod's father, Antipater, was an Idumean, a member of a fierce, desert-dwelling non-Jewish tribe living to the south of Judea. He married an Arabian woman named Cypros. They had four sons—Phasael, Herod, Joseph, and Pheroras—and one daughter, Salome. Antipater, who was wealthy and influential, seemed to have a knack for coming out on the winning side of things in the complicated series of conflicts between these Roman rivals as he rose to power. He wisely supported Julius Caesar in the civil war with Pompey. In 47 BC, Caesar rewarded Antipater with Roman citizenship, granted him freedom from taxes, and appointed him procurator of Judea. This imposition of a foreign ruler over Judea, with its capital, Jerusalem, was the beginning of troubles that plagued Herod his entire life. Nonetheless, we can see that his family was dealing at the highest levels of Roman power and influence in the country.

Herod the Great coin c. 40 BC

Antipater put his young son Herod, just twenty-six years old, over Galilee in 47 BC. Josephus describes Herod as physically strong, bold and fearless, an excellent horseman, and an indomitable fighter. Recall that in Galilee, Herod defeated a revolt led by Hezekiah, the father of the Galilean revolutionary Judas, one of our "three Messiahs" who arose after Herod's death in 4 BC, following in Hezekiah's footsteps.

Herod fell hopelessly in love with the Hasmonean Jewish princess Mariame, to whom he got engaged in 42 BC when she was still in her teens. Both her father, Alexander, and her mother, Alexandra, were grandchildren of Alexander Jannaeus, the Hasmonean priest who had ruled an independent Jewish state for twenty-seven years (103–76 BC), shortly before the Romans took over in 63 BC. Herod's motives to make Mariame his own went far beyond love, or even lust—though given her legendary beauty, and the wealth and influence of her aristocratic family, that was surely a factor. As it turned out, she was able to play him like a cithara. For Herod, such a charmed marriage would, in a back-door kind of way, provide him with a connection to the priestly family of the Hasmoneans, allowing him to father children of that honored lineage. To finalize the marriage, he divorced his wife Doris in 42 BC, removing his firstborn son, Antipater—whom he had named after his father—from his line of succession. Doris was from a Jewish family of Jerusalem with some standing—possibly even Davidic—and Herod, being a commoner, had married her to bolster his status as a "Jewish king." This would come back to haunt him right up to the week of his death, as neither Doris nor the disinherited Antipater ever forgave this humiliation. For the ensuing thirty-eight years, they plotted to regain the status Antipater thought rightly belonged to him as Herod's firstborn. These were bold, decisive moves by Herod, but they were only the beginning expressions of his desperate desire to find acceptance with the Jewish people.

It should be noted that Jesus's mother Mary had the same given name as Herod's new wife, Mariame—in fact, in our Greek New Testament Mary is regularly called Mariam

(Μαριὰμ), especially by Luke, even though our English translations use the more familiar Mary. This is a good example
of how translations sometimes obscure historical connections.
Mariam is a Hebrew form of the name that traces back to Miriam, the sister of Moses and Aaron, who was seen as a proph-
etess and a leader alongside her two brothers. As the prophet
Micah put it, talking about Israel's Exodus from Egypt: "I sent
before you Moses, Aaron, and Miriam" (Micah 6:4; Exodus
15:20). Strong women are a vital part of our story as it unfolds.

We noted earlier that the single ancient text we have that
mentions Mary's father, Joachim, says he was "an extremely rich
man." Joachim is described as owning property with abundant
flocks and lands. This would have put the family in a higher
level of their society. Mary is always piously pictured as a poor,
even illiterate peasant girl in the village of Nazareth, but the
status of her family might well have been quite the reverse. She
would have moved to Nazareth when her parents arranged
her engagement to Joseph—who presumably lived there, just
south of the metropolis. But growing up, she would have been
exposed to the culture of this urban center, undergoing an economic boom during Herod the Great's long rule. A landed
household would include servants and workers, exposure to the
diverse and cosmopolitan culture of Sepphoris, some measure
of education and literacy, and all the goings-on of an influential
Jewish household. She presumably had siblings, and her sister
is later mentioned, but not named, as one of those who came
from Galilee for that last Passover when Jesus was arrested and
crucified (John 19:25).

Even though the source in this case, the aforementioned
Protoevangelium of James, makes some dubious assertions
about Mary growing up a virgin in the temple in Jerusalem,
perhaps it reflects some accurate information about her family,
particularly if it can be correlated with other sources that might

indicate the same. This possibility is supported by a polemical rabbinic text from a later time that slanders Jesus and his mother, charging that "she who was the descendant *of princes and governors*, played the harlot with carpenters." This charge that Mary was sexually immoral is discussed later, but what is significant here is that her royal status seems to have been acknowledged even in slanderous gossip directed against her. Since the rabbis of this period want to denigrate Mary, giving her any kind of high status appears to be something they likely would not have mentioned unless it was generally known. I have previously noted Paul's statement that Jesus, although rich, *became poor*, and our indication that the Jesus movement was selling lands, houses, and possessions, and putting the funds in a common purse to support the group (2 Corinthians 8:9; Mark 10:29; Luke 9:58).

If Jesus and his family gave up everything for the sake of their mission, exhorting followers to do the same and adopting a voluntary form of communal living, this would explain their poverty. Jesus's brother James, as head of the Jerusalem community after Jesus's death, continued this practice, and the group is said to have followed his example (Acts 2:44–45). But this later practice, involving a large community of followers, would in no way detract from the upbringing that Mary had. And this cultural sophistication is reflected in dozens of stories in the Gospels where Jesus seems to be socially comfortable as a dinner guest of wealthy followers and has regular dealings with Roman military officers. In the Gospels he is pictured not as a villager, but as one who travels through the regions of major coastal cities like Tyre and Sidon as well as the great cities of the Decapolis east of the Jordan. I am convinced that these disparate threads point back to his mother, who had to have been a woman of stature and culture, given her family background.

Mary's family may well have been pleased that Joseph, despite

Joachim and Anna with Young Mary

her pregnancy, continued with his plans to marry her—if they ever even found out the child was not his. Both Matthew and Luke describe her as "his betrothed," not his wife, even at the birth of Jesus, so strictly speaking, she is an "unwed mother," since their marriage is not yet formalized (Matthew 1:18–25; Luke 2:5).

Herod's life is the quintessential tale of "the man who would be king." Even though the first half of his reign took place before Mary was born, her parents, Joachim and Anna, lived through the dangerous years of his rise to power, and so these events are more than relevant to Mary's background. In addition to those festival pilgrimages to Jerusalem, their life in Sepphoris was at the center of the political and military pulse of Galilee. Mary, even as a young girl, would have been acutely aware of the gripping drama that characterized Herod's life and times. The local Jewish population had become familiar with the young Herod and his bold, ruthless exploits in war when he was ruler over Galilee. Word traveled fast, in a matter of days, between Jerusalem and Galilee. The streets, markets, and dinner tables of Jewish Sepphoris were abuzz with gossip about Herod's extravagant ways.

As Herod rose to power, his most significant challenge was defeating his great rival Antigonus, the last of the Hasmonean rulers and the grandson of King Alexander Jannaeus. To complicate matters further, Antigonus was the uncle of the lovely Mariame, Herod's wife-to-be. Her father, Alexander, was his brother.

Antigonus had strong support from the populace as a native Jewish ruler with a revered and respected priestly lineage, and he knew Herod's weak spot was his lack of pedigree. He derided Herod as unfit to be king, a commoner, and as son of an Idumean convert, only a "half-Jew" from an Arab mother.

The Hasmonean Dynasty Over Five Generations
Showing the relationships of the leading family members

JOHN HYRCANUS (134–104 BC)
↓
ALEXANDER JANNAEUS (103–76 BC)
(*m.* SALOME ALEXANDRA, 76–67 BC)
↓
ARISTOBULUS II   HYRCANUS II
↓   ↘
ANTIGONUS II   ALEXANDRA (*m.* ALEXANDER)
↓
MARIAME (*m.* HEROD)

Antigonus was bitterly anti-Roman and had the support of the Parthians (or Persians) in the East—what is now modern

Iran. The Parthians backed his bid for native Jewish rulership of the country. The Roman interest was first and foremost stability on their eastern frontier, perpetually threatened by the Parthians. That means the Romans were prepared to oppose Antigonus with every ounce of power and strength they could muster. Having the young Herod as their ally and agent—even with his foreign ancestry—was a godsend. At least he had some claim to be Jewish, and now he had a Hasmonean princess at his side.

Herod declared all-out war on Antigonus. He had a good chance of becoming, at last, king of the Jews and drawing the popular support of the Jewish population. His model was Mariame's great-great-grandfather, the legendary John Hyrcanus, son of Simon the Maccabee, the first generation of native Jewish rulers since the Babylonian exile in the sixth century BC. John Hyrcanus had ruled the entire territory of the ancient land of Israel for thirty years (134–104 BC). His monumental tomb was one of the most prominent landmarks in the city of Jerusalem, just northwest of the famous Jaffa Gate. It was a kind of Lincoln Memorial of its day. The Romans desecrated it following the destruction of Jerusalem in AD 70, later turning the area into a shrine of the goddess Venus when the emperor Hadrian, in AD 135, rebuilt Jerusalem into a splendid Roman colony—Aelia Capitolina—dedicated to Jupiter.

Though far from having a lineage as distinguished as that of John Hyrcanus, Herod nonetheless saw himself as the ideal of a Jewish-Hellenistic ruler, someone compatible with the Romans while maintaining dynastic support from the Jewish populace. Also, the enemies of Hyrcanus had slandered him based on rumors that his mother had slept with a foreigner. Herod could take some small comfort in knowing that even the most distinguished of the Hasmonean rulers, who had the full support of the people, could be maligned as illegitimate. Herod saw his marriage to Mariame, John Hyrcanus's direct descendant, as almost equivalent to entering that distinguished family.

In 40 BC Marc Antony appointed Herod and his brother Phasael tetrarchs of Judea over the protests of several thousand Jews who gathered in opposition. These opponents were attacked and scattered by Roman-backed forces. Shortly after that, Parthian forces in Galilee captured Phasael and his favored priest Hyrcanus, a grandson of John Hyrcanus, who supported Herod and the Romans against Antigonus. The Parthians delivered these two prize captives to Antigonus in chains. Herod, upon hearing of his brother's capture, fled Jerusalem by night with his family, heading back home to his native land of Idumea, south of Judea in the Negev Desert. On the way, he had to fight off both Parthians and Jewish supporters of Antigonus. Arriving at the fortress of Masada, along the shores of the Dead Sea, Herod was joined by his brother Joseph. He left eight hundred of his men to guard the women and his household servants and went on to Petra in Arabia.

Back in Jerusalem, the move to put Antigonus on the throne drew strong support from the populace, which yearned for a native Hasmonean ruler who would oppose the foreign rule of Rome. Those in Galilee, who were overwhelmingly pro-Hasmonean, rejoiced that one of their own nation, the last of the Maccabean line of priests, was ruling in Jerusalem, and that the holy temple, the focus of the religious expression of Judaism, was in Jewish hands.

Josephus reports that Antigonus personally "bit off the ears" of Hyrcanus the high priest—his uncle, who had been backed by the Romans—so he could never serve again as high priest, since any such physical defects disqualified one from the office according to the Torah (Leviticus 21:17–23). This has to be one of the most macabre incidents of the time, illustrating the passions driving these two rivals for the throne. But there is more: to prevent Antigonus from torturing him, Phasael, though shackled, took his own life by dashing his head against a stone. The mutilated priest Hyrcanus was spared, but he was sent off to Parthia to serve as a bargaining chip in future dealings with Herod and his Roman patrons.

Before making his next move, Herod set out for Rome by way of Egypt in the winter of 40 BC. He received a grand reception from Cleopatra in Alexandria and sailed on to Rome, even though it was midwinter, when most shipping ceased due to storms. He was determined to see Marc Antony and Octavian, who were allied in the civil war against Brutus and Cassius following the assassination of Julius Caesar in 44 BC. Herod was received with honor and accolades by both Antony and Octavian—the future emperor Augustus—who convened the Senate and had him declared king of Judea. Herod was just thirty-three years old—ironically, the exact age of Jesus when he was mockingly crucified as "king of the Jews" by the Romans.

Chapter Five

THAT OTHER KING
OF THE JEWS

Are you the king of the Jews?

—Pontius Pilate

Antony and Octavian, the two most powerful men in the world at that moment, escorted Herod arm in arm through the Roman Forum to offer sacrifices at the temple of Jupiter. Antony sponsored a lavish banquet, in full Roman style, in Herod's honor, celebrating the first day of his reign. Herod at long last had achieved the legitimacy he longed for from the Romans, but to the Jewish people, who despised Roman rule, he remained a usurper who must be deposed by a legitimate king of Davidic ancestry. Herod's task now was to consolidate his rule in the land of Israel and eliminate all rival claims to native kingship. It was this dynamic that shaped Mary's world and led to the crucifixion of her firstborn son as a rival heir to that throne.

Herod hurried back to Judea in 39 BC with the backing of his own Jewish loyalists and a Roman legion at his command. In his absence, Antigonus, his royal rival for the throne, had laid siege to Masada, attempting to capture Herod's family, but he withdrew on news of Herod's return from Rome. Herod then marched to Galilee, delaying a siege of Jerusalem until he controlled the north. He secured Sepphoris, the capital of the region, with overwhelming Roman-backed forces and routed his opponents.

Josephus relates one story that dramatically illustrates the extent of the opposition to Herod the Great's rule among much of the populace. As Herod conducted his cleanup campaign in Galilee, Jewish supporters of Antigonus had fortified themselves in the many caves along the cliffs of Mount Arbel, which towered twelve hundred feet above the northern edge of the Sea of Galilee, refusing to surrender. One individual, who had his wife and seven sons with him, was adamant in his defiance.

Mount Arbel, overlooking the Sea of Galilee

From below, Herod begged the man to give up and promised him amnesty and safety while the man shouted curses at him, accusing him of being a "lowborn upstart" with no right to be the Jewish king. One by one, the man ordered his own children to come to the mouth of the cave, where he executed them in plain sight of Herod and his forces and pushed their bodies to the ground below. Finally, he killed his wife, shoved her body out of the cave, and jumped after her, crushing his skull against the rocks.

Today the cliffs of Arbel overlook one of the most beautiful scenes on the Sea of Galilee, with Magdala, the home of Mary Magdalene, and Capernaum, where Jesus and his family made their headquarters, just below. I have climbed those dizzying cliffs with my students, exploring the caves where this appalling scene unfolded. This family's fanaticism makes full sense in the context of the zealous messianic expectations of that time. Since this bloody story was passed on by Josephus decades later, we can be sure it was told and retold over the years in Jewish households all over Galilee. Anyone coming from Sepphoris or Nazareth or any of the villages of that area to the Sea of Galilee has to pass below the Arbel cliffs through a narrow valley leading to the shores. The Gospel of John specifically mentions Jesus, along with his mother and brothers, passing this area on their way to Capernaum, where Peter and Andrew lived on the northwest shore of the Sea of Galilee (John 2:12). Jesus would have made that journey countless times over his lifetime. Such a dramatic tale, known to Josephus when he was growing up in the 40s AD, is a good illustration of how such accounts of the early days of Herod the Great circulated among the people throughout Mary's life.

Herod had put his brother Joseph in charge of the forces in Judea until he could secure Galilee, ordering him to make no move on his own against Antigonus. As the summer of 38 BC

arrived, Joseph decided he would march to Jericho to seques-
ter the ripening grain crop. In Jerusalem, thirteen miles to the
west, Antigonus got word of this plan and attacked Joseph,
destroying his inexperienced Roman forces. Joseph was killed
in the battle, and Antigonus decapitated his corpse, rejecting
the pleas of Herod's family to retrieve it for burial according
to Jewish law.

Herod was as enraged as he was aggrieved by the brutal
deaths of two of his brothers—first Phasael and now Joseph.
Herod arrived in Jericho and prepared for the siege of Jerusalem, more determined than ever to utterly crush his archenemy
Antigonus. He began securing the countryside village by village, taking what he needed and killing any who opposed his
rule. The populace was divided between supporters of Herod
and those of Antigonus. Herod lay siege to Jerusalem in the
spring of 37 BC, three years after he had been proclaimed king
in Rome. During the assault, which lasted three months, Herod
went to Samaria and married Mariame, by then seventeen, in
preparation for his victory over Antigonus in Jerusalem. Once
again, he wanted to enter the city with the Hasmonean princess
by his side, knowing that could potentially sway the populace
to support him. While Mariame's family was divided in their
support for Rome, she must have felt that marrying the king
would be advantageous to her own fortunes.

The stakes could not have been higher for Antigonus and
his forces, but, lacking food and reinforcements, they were
hardly a match for Herod's army, now backed by a legion of
battle-hardened Roman troops. In the end, Herod breached
the city walls and decisively defeated them, executing those who
had been most loyal to Antigonus and hoping those he spared
would recognize his Roman-backed rule.

Herod was careful to capture Antigonus alive, thinking he
could better garner the support of those left in Jerusalem if

he turned him over to the Romans rather than making a spectacle of him in front of the populace. Josephus tells us that Antigonus was small in stature compared to the robust Herod, who gleefully mocked his rival, calling him by the feminine name Antigone, implying he was a weakling. Herod sent him in chains to Antony in Antioch, who had him first crucified, the most shameful possible punishment, and then beheaded, as a final indignity. Herod surely was thinking of his brother Joseph, whose head Antigonus had displayed and refused to return for burial. The grisly death of Antigonus in 37 BC ended 126 years of independent Hasmonean rule over the country. A new era had dawned, and Roman power prevailed.

In 1971, construction workers building a private home just north of the Old City uncovered a rock-hewn tomb with two rooms connected by a passageway. The tomb had apparently been looted in antiquity, but two exceptionally beautiful ossuaries—limestone bone boxes—remained, one in a sealed locus, likely overlooked by the thieves. Incised on the wall of the smaller room was a seven-line inscription in Paleo-Hebrew script, the archaic style of writing used by the Hasmoneans on their coins to reflect their patriotic commitment to Jewish independence and self-rule. The inscription was carefully removed from the tomb and is now on display in the Rockefeller Museum in Jerusalem.

Antigonus's ossuary, royally decorated

It is written in the first person by one Abba, a priest who relates that he buried "Matatai son of Judah"—Antigonus's Hebrew name—in the cave that he bought with a deed. One of the skeletons showed marks of crucifixion and beheading, including crucifixion nails, put through the hands, still fused to the bones. At first, the skeleton was identified as a woman's, but anthropologists at Tel Aviv University concluded it was that of a man of slight stature, explaining Herod's mocking of Antigonus as Antigone.

In 2016, I was invited to participate in a PBS documentary titled *Last Days of Jesus,* which dealt with Roman crucifixion, produced by Simcha Jacobovici. As part of that research, we did paleo-DNA testing of a bone sample taken from the well-preserved Antigonus jawbone, giving us a clear reading of the mtDNA that he inherited from his mother. Since Jewish priests normally married women of related priestly families—in this case the royal Hasmonean clan—it is very likely we have a DNA sample of the royal Hasmonean dynasty.

There is a final ironic twist to Antigonus's story. Josephus reports that Antipater—Herod's firstborn son, whose mother, Doris, Herod had banished so he could marry the Hasmonean Mariame—took one of Antigonus's daughters as his wife. Antipater, much like his father, hoped that wedding a Hasmonean princess would solidify his own popularity with the Jewish populace and increase his chance of succeeding his father as king of the Jews.

Despite Herod's consolidation of power, he could not seem to control his fits of jealousy toward Mariame's Hasmonean family. Mariame had a younger brother named Jonathan, whom Herod started to see as a potential rival. It was one thing to marry a Hasmonean woman, but quite another to protect and nurture a male of such distinguished Jewish ancestry. What followed is one of the most shocking episodes in Herod's reign.

Although this happened in the year 35 BC, fifteen years before Mary's birth, its implications would surely have haunted Mary throughout her life, since she carried the genetic lineage that put her and her children at risk.

Alexandra, the ambitious mother of Mariame and Jonathan, was determined that Herod should make Jonathan the high priest, the second-most-powerful spot in the government, next to the king himself. Jonathan would then be well poised to make a bid for the Hasmonean family kingship to be restored—a possibility that Herod feared more than anything else. Josephus relates that a friend of Marc Antony's, Quintus Delius, visited Jerusalem and was so impressed by the charm and beauty of both Jonathan and Mariame that he persuaded Alexandra to send portraits of the two to Antony and Cleopatra in Egypt. Delius described the siblings extravagantly, saying that they seemed almost to be the progeny of the gods. Alexandra, elated at the idea, commissioned paintings to send to Antony, hoping he would invite them to visit Egypt, thus gaining power over Herod, into whose family they were being drawn.

Marc Antony declined to ask for Mariame, since she was Herod's wife, but he did request that Jonathan be sent—presumably to satisfy his fondness for beautiful young boys. Herod, however, wanted to keep Jonathan under his thumb. He worried that if the boy left the country, the whole land would fall into disorder and rebellion, since the Jews hoped to overturn the government and restore a Hasmonean king.

Herod decided to make Jonathan high priest, perhaps as a way of controlling things and preventing a palace coup. He had grown suspicious of Alexandra's plotting, so he put her under palace arrest lest she attempt to meddle behind his back with Antony and Cleopatra. When Alexandra wrote to Cleopatra to beg for help, Cleopatra urged her to escape to Egypt secretly with Jonathan, promising she would take their side with Antony to help restore their family dynasty. At this juncture, the entire future of Herod's hopes and dreams to be king of the Jews hung in the balance.

Alexandra had two coffins made with the plan that she and Jonathan would be smuggled out of the city under cover of night by trusted servants who would transport them to the coast to board a waiting ship for Egypt. Anyone who died in the city had to be removed within twenty-four hours, so coffins being carried at night to burial sites would not raise suspicions. When Herod got word of the plot, he allowed it to proceed so he could catch Alexandra in the act. He seized the two coffins before they could be loaded onto the ship but then pretended to pardon her treachery so he could keep her under his control.

At the Festival of Tabernacles, or Sukkot, in the fall of that year, Jonathan, not yet eighteen years old, presided at the religious rites in the temple. Tall and handsome, he was resplendently dressed in the magnificent linen garments of the high priest. When the crowds of Jewish worshippers saw him, they burst into tears, shouting accolades to this native son whose beauty only underscored his royal pedigree as a Hasmonean. Herod was insanely jealous, fearing that the crowd was becoming a mob that would demand his brother-in-law be made king of the Jews in his place.

After the festival, Alexandra hosted a feast at the royal palace at Jericho for Herod and the family. Herod behaved warmly toward Jonathan, giving him encouragement to keep drinking. As the heat of the day began to wane, Herod suggested the young men cool themselves in the palace swimming pool. A group of Herod's friends and servants began to roughhouse with Jonathan, at first playfully and then more forcefully,

The Jericho pool where Herod drowned Jonathan

pushing his head under water as he thrashed about and struggled to free himself. In a game that turned deadly by design, Jonathan was held under water until he drowned.

Word of Jonathan's death spread quickly throughout Jerusalem and north to Galilee. The entire country was dazed with grief. Even though Jonathan was not the Roman-appointed king of the Jews, having him as the high priest had been a monumental boost to their sense of autonomy.

Herod feigned horror while Alexandra and Mariame were inconsolable. Neither of them believed the boy's death had been accidental. Josephus observes that, as Mariame's hatred for Herod grew, his passion for her increased all the more, but he had clearly destroyed any feelings she might have had for him. Herod arranged a lavish funeral for Jonathan, but Alexandra could think only of revenge. She wrote to Cleopatra, urging Antony to avenge the murder. Antony demanded that Herod meet him on the Syrian border to clear himself of suspicion. Herod left his sister Salome's husband, Joseph, in charge in Jerusalem, and secretly gave him orders to kill Mariame if he did not return. Herod preferred to have his wife dead rather than in the arms of another man, particularly Antony, whom he suspected of lusting after her.

While Herod was away, rumors spread throughout the city that Antony had had Herod tortured and put to death. Alexandra began to make her plans. She and Mariame would flee the city and ask protection of the Roman legion outside Jerusalem while sending word to Antony, who she was sure had an ardent interest in Mariame. This was a calculating but shrewd move, since Antony had thirteen legions stationed in Syria at his command. With Antony's favor, Alexandra was hoping that the Hasmonean throne could be restored with her as the queen mother. She was well aware that her grandmother and namesake, Salome Alexandra, the widow of Alexander Jannaeus, had ruled the land as queen after her husband's death.

In the meantime, messengers brought word from Herod reporting that he was alive and well. He had successfully defended himself before Antony and had given Cleopatra a palm-tree plantation in Jericho, as well as wealthy lands in several nearby towns, to appease her. Upon his return, his sister Salome told him that Mariame had been sleeping with Joseph in his absence. Salome was terribly jealous of Mariame, who often berated her for her low family origins in contrast to her own. Herod also learned that Mariame had sent her portrait to Antony while he was away. Herod was enraged, but was finally persuaded to accept Mariame's denials of adultery. Still, he ordered Joseph executed based on his lingering doubts and considered killing Salome as well, until his anger subsided. Herod also put Alexandra in chains, persuaded that she too was involved in this would-be palace coup.

For many years I passed by Jericho, which is just north of the Dead Sea, thirteen miles from Jerusalem, on my way to Qumran, where the Dead Sea Scrolls were found. Jericho is the lowest spot on earth, thirteen hundred feet below sea level, and touted as one of the oldest cities in the world. About a day's horseback ride from Jerusalem, it has warm and pleasant winters. I had visited the ancient town, but never explored the excavations of Herod's winter palace complex, situated below the Judean cliffs on both sides of the refreshing springs of Wadi Qelt. The Hasmoneans had initially built a palace there, with a defensive tower and civic center, but Herod had enlarged the whole complex in stages. The excavations reveal the opulent lifestyle at court, with colorful frescoes, elaborate mosaics, baths and fountains, lavishly furnished rooms, and expansive gardens.

Recently, I spent an hour walking around the Hasmonean-period ruins, including the enormous, partitioned swimming pool, now exposed, that was likely the scene of Jonathan's drowning. As the desert sun slipped below the horizon, I recalled Josephus's vivid description of that day. The pool is of course empty today, so I went down the steps to the bottom to get a feel for its depth. It was one of those rare moments when one connects a physical place with a historical event one can only read about. I drove back to Jerusalem feeling I had stepped into a kind of time machine that took me back into Mary's world.

Those were brutal times, especially for members of the Hasmonean priestly family. A few years earlier, Alexander, the father of Mariame and Jonathan, was beheaded on orders of the Roman general Pompey, rival of Julius Caesar. Their grandfather the high priest Aristobulus was poisoned by supporters of Pompey who had his corpse preserved in honey until Marc Antony finally was able to send it back to Jerusalem for a royal burial.

When Herod's two sons with Mariame, Alexander and

Aristobulus, were children, he fawned over them. They represented a kind of shoring-up of his legitimacy, given the distinguished pedigree of their mother. He sent them to Rome for an imperial education and provided lavishly for them. The emperor Augustus favored Herod, second only to Marcus Agrippa, who was his closest friend and confidant. But clearly, not all was well in this new royal household, despite Herod's excessive wealth and Roman patronage.

As the years passed, Herod once again began to be tormented by suspicions that Mariame was unfaithful to him. She vehemently denied these accusations, and Herod went back and forth, first believing her, then doubting her again. Mariame's old antagonist, Herod's sister Salome, once again incriminated her, and this time she was joined by Mariame's own mother, Alexandra, who had decided that getting her beautiful daughter out of the way might increase her own odds of replacing Herod. Mariame had stopped sleeping with Herod after Jonathan's murder, and despite his pleas and declarations of love, she would not relent. This only drove Herod to the boiling point, and he became crazed with jealousy. Josephus, who reports all this based on his contemporary sources, insists that Mariame was innocent and Herod's suspicions were groundless. Mariame was also distraught that Herod had executed her elderly uncle Hyrcanus, for whom she had great affection, though he was no threat since the disfigurement of his ears by Antigonus had rendered him unfit to serve again as high priest.

At last, in desperation, Herod ordered Mariame put on trial with the charge that she had prepared a love potion to poison him—apparently a baseless accusation. Although the court decreed a sentence of death, Herod at first only had her imprisoned, unwilling to see the sentence carried out. Finally, with Salome pressuring him to consent to the recommendation of his own court and assuring him of Mariame's treachery, he had to accept the events he'd set in motion. We are not told how the sentence was carried out, but presumably she was beheaded. Herod's beloved Mariame was dead. Herod was forty-four years old. They had been married for only eight years.

To his dying day, Herod regretted having Mariame killed. Josephus writes that he tried to forget his loss through hunting and banqueting, but fell ill in Samaria, where he was haunted by memories of their wedding. He would wander his palace at night, moaning and weeping, and calling out her name. He began to neglect all affairs of state.

Sensing Herod's instability, Alexandra made the move she had been waiting for. She pronounced Herod unfit to reign because of insanity and declared herself queen. Her plan was to groom her two grandsons, Alexander and Aristobulus, to take over in the future, thus restoring the Hasmonean dynasty to power. This threat served to shake Herod out of his grief, and he ordered Alexandra executed in 29 BC.

In Herod's first will, he had made Alexander and Aristobulus his heirs, knowing they had favor with Augustus and were beloved of the people. By the year 12 BC, he began to quarrel with the boys, and in 7 BC, roughly two years before Jesus's birth, Herod had them both strangled at his palace at Sebaste in Samaria. This decisive move essentially cleared the board of all possible rivals from the revered Hasmonean bloodline, into which Herod had married. Ironically, Herod had largely destroyed the family he'd so desperately sought to draw close to. He was to die just three years later, so the matter of a loyal heir intensified his desperation.

All told, the list of Hasmoneans who were killed by the time Mary was twelve years old is staggering. All of these deaths were related to one issue—who would legitimately rule as king and/or high priest of the Jewish people?

- Aristobulus, son of Alexander Jannaeus and Salome Alexander (48 BC)
- Alexander, father of Mariame and husband of Alexandra (48 BC)
- Antigonus, defeated by Herod, executed by Marc Antony (37 BC)
- Jonathan, brother of Mariame and son of Alexandra and Alexander (36 BC)
- Hyrcanus, son of Alexander Jannaeus and Salome Alexander (30 BC)
- Mariame, wife of Herod, daughter of Alexandra and Alexander (29 BC)
- Alexander, son of Herod and Mariame (7 BC)
- Aristobulus, son of Herod and Mariame (7 BC)

Besides Doris and Mariame, Herod married eight other times, sometimes for love, mostly for political reasons, and had fourteen other children whose names have been preserved. He even married another Mariame, the daughter of a high priest named Shimon, in a futile attempt to gain some semblance of legitimacy. The only surviving Hasmonean of the older generation was an unnamed daughter of his archrival Antigonus, whom Herod's son Antipater had married.

Herod vacillated on the question of who would succeed him. He had half a dozen wills, naming at various times different sons as heir, including his firstborn, Antipater, then Philip, Herod II, Archelaus, and Herod Antipas. Herod seemed initially to favor Antipater, perhaps thinking the eldest was more appropriate for his own abortive "dynasty." As a further sign of favor, he gave Antipater the daughter of his murdered son Aristobulus as a second wife—again hoping to shore up some kind of legitimacy for his bloodline and thus indirectly ensuring it for Herod's potential grandchildren through Antipater. In the end, the whole plan fell apart. Herod became bitterly envious of Antipater and, five days before his own death, ordered him executed.

Herod died in the spring of 4 BC. His death was prolonged and miserable. Josephus reports that he suffered from a raging fever, tumors in his feet, inflammation of the abdomen from worms, gangrene, asthma, and convulsions. Toward the end, his only relief was sitting in the hot springs at Callirrhoe, on the eastern shore of the Dead Sea, below the fortress of Machaerus. Some years ago I took several of my students to this precise area. Those thermal springs are still scalding hot and the desert oasis still lush. We all sat in the shallow pools, with steam rising from the water that fills the terraced stone basins in the bedrock, vividly trying to imagine the sick and aged Herod in that very spot.

Reportedly, the emperor Augustus once said, "It is better to be Herod's pig than his son"—the joke being that, since Herod was a Jew and didn't eat pork, a pig would have a better chance of surviving than a son. By all measures, Herod was a cruel and oppressive tyrant. He is remembered as a great builder of cities, palaces, harbors, monuments, fortresses, and temples—but even those accomplishments were made possible only by his murderous grasp for power, his oppressive taxation, and the thousands of slaves he kept in bondage.

Herod's kingdom was divided among three of his sons, and the emperor Augustus endorsed this move. Archelaus would rule over Judea, Antipas over Galilee, and Philip over Perea (Transjordan) and outlying areas to the east. Antipas, in particular, was the most like his father—bound and determined to become king of the Jews over the whole realm.

These stories were told and retold throughout the land over the next decades, shaping Mary's world as she matured into womanhood with a family of her own. As Jesus, James, and the other children grew up, these tales had to have been as real to them as the present. In fact, it seemed in the case of Herod Antipas that history might be repeating itself. Antipas longed to emulate his father on every level. Years later, when Jesus was told that Herod Antipas was hunting him down, intending to kill him, Jesus replied defiantly, "Go tell that fox that I must finish the course I have been given" (Luke 13:32). It was, of course, Herod Antipas who beheaded John the Baptizer, with whom Jesus had grown up and whom he loved. Jesus refused even to speak to him on the night before his crucifixion—though Herod questioned him at length—and it was Herod's soldiers who mocked him as a "king" by putting one of Herod's royal purple robes on him, repeating the same kind of mockery that his father, Herod the Great, had once dished out to Antigonus, his chief rival (Luke 23:6–16).

The New Testament opens with Matthew's story about Herod the Great, shortly before his death, ordering the slaughter of all the male children in Bethlehem and in the region who were two years old or under in a futile attempt to murder Mary's firstborn. This so-called Slaughter of the Innocents has become one of the centerpieces of any Christmas story. Historians consider it a fabricated legend. We have very detailed records of Herod's reign, especially from Josephus. Neither he nor any other contemporary source mentions such an event. Herod was ruthless, that is certain, but this sort of systematic, house-to-house mass slaughter of all male children of the region is inconceivable. Herod would have never dared such a thing under the watchful eye of Augustus, whose Pax Romana was a hallmark of his rule. Such a move would have sparked a massive revolt among the Jewish populace—the last thing Herod wanted. Most scholars think that Matthew is echoing themes from Exodus, in which the infant Moses is saved from the slaughter of all male Jewish children ordered by the pharaoh

(Exodus 1:15–2:10). As Moses was protected from death and later led the Israelites out of Egyptian slavery, so too would Jesus be protected and save his people from their sins.

The irony here is that Matthew's legendary story nonetheless reflects a core historical reality about Herod's reign. He went to extreme lengths opposing any vestige of indigenous hereditary rule, including murdering members of his own family whom he considered a threat to his position. It's unlikely that he ever knew of the young Mary and her newborn son. She was only fifteen when he died, but as she held her baby in her arms and the good news of Herod's death spread, resulting in messianic revolts all over the country, Herod's son Antipas, who would devastate her family with his own murderous quest for legitimacy, was poised in the wings.

Chapter Six

MARY'S SECRET

For that which is conceived in her is of the Holy
Spirit

—Angel of the Lord

There are two different accounts of Jesus's birth in the
New Testament, one from Matthew, the other from
Luke. Both clearly assert that Joseph is *not* the biological father of Jesus. Luke narrates Mary's side of things, whereas
Matthew relates things from Joseph's perspective, but the point
is the same: Mary's pregnancy is "of the Holy Spirit," during
her engagement to Joseph, and he is not the father.

There are numerous tales in Greek and Roman literature
about "divine beings"—heroes, philosophers, or demigods—
whose conceptions were attributed to a god impregnating their
mother. The long list includes Hercules, with his marvelous
feats of strength; Plato and his wisdom; Alexander the Great,
conqueror of the known world; and Apollonius of Tyana, with
his wonder-working powers. These sorts of legends are found
throughout ancient cultures, whether Greek, Roman, Egyptian,
or Hebrew, and their clear purpose is to emphasize the extraordinary significance of the child born. The ancient world did
not share our biological understanding of pregnancy and birth.

Miracles were part of everyday lives and miraculous tales of conceptions and births were common. These two accounts in Luke and Matthew of Mary's pregnancy *"of the Holy Spirit"* can easily be read in this broader cultural context. As such they can be understood less as scientific reports and more as ways of affirming God's special destiny for Mary's firstborn son, Jesus.

The seduction of Alkmene, mother
of Hercules, by Zeus

And yet, we find hints of a much less mythological take on Mary's pregnancy. In the Gospel of John, when Jesus speaks of God as his father, he is sarcastically attacked by some of his enemies, who declare to him, "We were not born of fornication, we have one Father, even God" (John 8:41). They are evidently picking up on the local gossip that Mary's pregnancy was not from Joseph. They also call Jesus a "Samaritan," in the same context, implying his father was of questionable pedigree (John 8:48). The second-century-AD Christian writer Tertullian, who is considered the founder of Latin theology, has an interesting passage in which he imagines how Jesus's enemies will be punished on the Day of Judgment for saying he was "the son of a carpenter or the harlot, a Sabbath breaker, a Samaritan and a demon-possessed man . . ."

There is something oddly irregular about Jesus's birth hinted at in Matthew's account. He rather strangely includes four women in his genealogy—Tamar, Rahab, Ruth, and Bathsheba— when such male lineages almost never include women (Matthew 1:3–6). Each of the four is known for some kind of questionable sexual behavior, but all are connected to prominent men of the direct lineage of King David. It is as if Matthew wants to hint to the reader: don't be too quick to judge Mary for her pregnancy, God used these other women connected to the house of David in major ways, despite the irregular nature of their pregnancies. At the same time Matthew makes it clear that Joseph, whose line he is tracing, is the husband of Mary, but not the father of Jesus (Matthew 1:16). Luke has something quite similar. He begins his genealogy with the assertion that Jesus was "supposedly" of Joseph (Luke 3:23). Although the theologically embellished birth narratives in Matthew and Luke develop a generation after Jesus, they preserve a historical core: Mary becomes pregnant before her marriage to Joseph, and Joseph is not the father.

These implications, or outright charges, of illegitimacy are not limited to the New Testament Gospels. There is good reason to think this slander might have dogged Jesus and Mary their entire lives. It seems to just pop up, here and there. The Coptic Gospel of Thomas, a text that dates to the early second century, was discovered in 1945 among the Nag Hammadi codices in a jar in the sands of Egypt. It consists of a collection of 114 sayings of Jesus, most of which are not included in our New Testament Gospels. Saying 105 is the most interesting in this regard: "Jesus said: He who shall know his father and mother shall be called the son of a harlot." This can also be translated as a question: "Will they call him the son of a harlot?" The implication seems to be that Mary's pregnancy with Jesus could be seen in a negative way.

The Jewish term for a child born of any illicit sexual relationship outside of engagement or marriage is *mamzer*, often mistakenly translated as "bastard," but it is a legal term, not a term of profanity in Hebrew. A related term the rabbis use is a "hushling" or "silenced one." This is someone who knows his mother but not his father. There is also the term "foundling," used for one who knows neither father nor mother. However, any child born to an engaged or married woman is presumed to be her husband's, unless she is so promiscuous that such a presumption becomes unsupportable. Accordingly, much depends on the man, and how he decides to handle the pregnancy. In Matthew's account of Joseph discovering his fiancée's pregnancy, we are explicitly told that Joseph did not make it public—he went ahead with the marriage, taking the child as his own, "unwilling to put her to shame" (Matthew 1:19–25). Legally speaking, Jesus then becomes his legitimate child.

The Jewish Mishnah, compiled in the third century AD, quotes a saying from Rabbi Simeon ben Azzai, an early-second-century rabbi, that some take to refer to Jesus, or if not to him directly, to one of a similarly questionable birth: "I found a family register in Jerusalem and in it was written 'Such-a-one is a *mamzer* through [transgression of] your neighbor's wife.'" The use of the term "such-a-one" to avoid using the name of a controversial person is attested elsewhere. There is an oblique reference in the Babylonian Talmud mentioned previously that likely refers to Mary as well: "She who was the descendant of princes and governors played the harlot with carpenters." This persistent theme, charging Mary with an illicit union, is found dozens of times in various strata of rabbinic sources over a period of several hundred years.

The same idea surfaces in the Qur'an, where we read of "a great slander" against Mary, referring to Jesus as "illegitimate," rather than God "casting into Mary" a spirit causing her pregnancy (4:156, 171; 19:16–36).

Matthew quotes a text from the prophet Isaiah that has been taken for centuries by Christians as a prediction of Jesus's virgin birth: "Behold, a virgin shall conceive and bear a son, and his name shall be called Emmanuel (which means, God with us)" (Matthew 1:23).

The original Hebrew word in Isaiah is 'almah, translated as "young woman" in modern translations. The idea is that a young woman or maiden of marriageable age will have a child, and that child would become a "sign" of God's special presence. Read in its historical context, this verse, Isaiah 7:14, is referring to the divinely sanctioned birth of a normal child in Isaiah's time—the seventh century BC—to a young woman of that time. The birth of this child, which in context appears to be Isaiah's, was to be a sign to Ahaz, the king of Judah, assuring him that God would protect Jerusalem from an imminent invasion by the Assyrians. Matthew wants to convey the idea that in the case of Mary and Jesus, her child too will be a sign to her generation—bringing deliverance to the Jewish people. That is clearly Matthew's meaning, and his explicit reference to four women of questionable sexual reputation in the royal line of King David underlines that point.

So who might Jesus's father have been—assuming it was not Joseph? Do we have a name or even a hint of such a person? And if so, what do we know about him? As it turns out, there

Fifteenth-century sculpture of Mary
and the Infant Jesus, Tuscany

is a name in some of our earliest Jewish sources, where we have references to Mary's son as "Jesus son of Pantera." But who might Pantera have been?

This name, Pantera, has commonly been explained as a slanderous pun. Since the Christians were hailing Jesus as son of the "Virgin" (*parthenos*), his Jewish and Greco-Roman enemies were sportingly calling him son of the "Panther" (*panthera*). Panthers were known for their sexual prowess, so such a pun was intended to be humorously crude, implying that Jesus's father was a lusty beast. But this usage is never found in any ancient text, even by the most avowed enemies of Christianity. It was first suggested in the nineteenth century.

In the earliest examples we have of this name, Jesus is routinely identified as "Yeshua ben Pantera"—Jesus, son of Pantera—without any pejorative connotation whatsoever. The name is simply given in passing: a son identified by his father's

name, as common and innocuous as the New Testament desig-
nations "Jesus, son of Joseph" or "Simon, son of Jonah," referring to Peter. These random references come from the close of
the first century and the beginning of the second, with stories
of rabbis encountering some of Jesus's followers just a generation removed from him. These earlier rabbinic references are
not focused on the name Pantera, nor do they imply anything
scandalous about Mary's pregnancy. It is a real name that was
known among Jews and non-Jews of the time, and directly
identifying his father. What's more, these earliest stories about
Jesus, son of Pantera, are set in the streets of Sepphoris in the
late first century, fewer than four miles northwest of Nazareth.
These are local traditions circulating and passed on by those
who lived in the region. This confluence of time and place is
rather extraordinary.

One example is when a certain Rabbi Eleazar ben Dama was
bitten by a snake. A man named Jacob of Sikhnaya (or Sikhnin)
came to heal him "in the name of Yeshua ben Pantera." Rabbi
Ishmael, who headed the Pharisees, objected, since Jesus, or
Yeshua, was seen as a heretic by the rabbis. Before the two rabbis could settle their debate, Rabbi Eleazar died. Rabbi Ishmael
attributed his death to giving credence to a figure like Jesus,
who had opposed the Pharisees, but there is no hint that the
description "son of Pantera" was in any way being used in a
pejorative way. It is simply a patronymic. In another example,
one Eliezer, a prominent rabbi of the late first century, was
walking on the streets of Sepphoris and met a man named
Jacob of Sikhnin, who told him about a teaching of a certain
Yeshua ben Pantera. This teaching involved a technical question of Jewish law: What was to be done with money brought
to the house of God that had been earned by a prostitute? Jesus
had said it should be received as other gifts were, but used to
build toilets and bath houses, pointing out that "from filth it

came and to filth it should go," quoting Micah 1:7. The answer pleased Eliezar very much—and for that he was arrested on suspicion of sympathizing with heretics, since the teachings of Jesus, however wise or appealing, were anathema to the rabbis at that time.

These two sources are set in the generation after Jesus, in Galilee, on the streets of Sepphoris, and Jesus is regularly called the "son of Pantera," with no aspersions implied. This is our earliest and most important clue in tracking down the possible historical connection of the name Pantera with Jesus. What Jesus, son of Pantera is reputed to have taught in the case of the wages of a prostitute is good Jewish legal jurisprudence.

This makes it clear that these two Jewish groups—the Pharisees and the Nazarenes—were bitterly opposed to one another, with the former denouncing the latter as heretics. The various sects of Judaism of the late first century were hopelessly divided; in fact, the rabbis say that Jerusalem was destroyed because of the "baseless hatred" within the parties and the Jewish body politic itself.

These earliest references to Pantera stand in contrast to several dozen much later references in rabbinic literature that slanderously charged Jesus was the illegitimate son of a man named Pantera, with whom his mother had committed adultery. It was this story that got passed on beyond Jewish circles. The main example is the late-second-century philosopher Celsus, in an anti-Christian work titled *On the True Doctrine*. In one section, Celsus imagines asking Jesus about the true origins of his birth, questioning the "cover-up" stories related by Matthew and Luke in their Gospels:

Let us imagine what a Jew—let alone a philosopher— might put to Jesus: "Is it not true, good sir, that you fabricated the story of your birth from a virgin to quiet

rumors about the true and unsavory circumstances
of your origins? Is it not the case that far from being
born in royal David's city of Bethlehem, you were born
in a poor country town, and of a woman who earned
her living by spinning? Is it not the case that when her
deceit was discovered, to wit, that she was pregnant
by a Roman soldier named Panthera, she was driven
away by her husband—the carpenter—and convicted
of adultery? Indeed, is it not so that in her disgrace,
wandering far from home, she gave birth to a male child
in silence and humiliation? What more?" (I:32)

Several early Christian writers, responding to these charges
that Jesus was the illegitimate "son of Pantera," a Roman soldier, counter with the explanation that the name Pantera was an
ancestral name in Jesus's family lineage, so it would be appro-
priately used, not as the name of his biological father but as a
designation of his general family ancestry. This would be similar to the way in which the term "Hasmonean" came to be used
for those descended from Hasmon, a forebear of this famous
priestly family. In that general sense, these Christian writers
claim, Jesus could be identified as a "son of Pantera"—again
not taking it as slanderous in any way, but simply as a family
name.

Epiphanius, an early-fourth-century Christian writer, claims
the name is from Joseph's side of the family. This is of course
possible, but less likely than a related claim. John of Damascus, a sixth-century church father, introduces the name into
the genealogy of Mary, stating that she was the daughter of
Joachim, who was the son of a certain Bar Panther, who was the
son of Levi, presumably surnamed Pantera. This same connection to Mary's family is echoed by other later Byzantine theologians. This is rather remarkable, as it would put the name

Pantera into Mary's royal/priestly line. The seventh-century Jewish Christian author of the *Teaching of Jacob* quotes a Jewish teacher from Tiberias who claims to know the genealogy of Mary. He writes that she is "the daughter of Joakim, and her mother was Anna. Now Joakim is son of Panther, and Panther was brother of Melchi, as the tradition of us Jews in Tiberias has it, of the seed of Nathan, the son of David, of the seed of Judah." It is difficult to imagine these Greek Christian writers making a place for the name Panthera (or Pantera) in the genealogical records of Mary unless they had warrant for it in Eastern Christian tradition. It does not surprise me that the name was completely lost in the West and became a symbol of slander, since Luke's genealogy of Mary was usually downplayed in favor of Matthew's royal line of David through Solomon.

Unfortunately, beyond this idea that Pantera is a name from the families of Mary and Joseph, who might well have been related, we have little to go on. There is a first-century Jewish tomb in Jerusalem with a Greek ossuary inscription that reads: *[Iō]sepou pentherou [Dr]osou.*

One could translate this inscription, "Of Joseph, father-in-law (or perhaps son-in-law) of Drosus." However, Tal Ilan prefers translating it as a proper name, either as "Of Joseph Penthera of Drosus" or "Of Joseph [who is] son of Penthera of Drosus," taking the name Penthera as equivalent to Pantera, and "Drosus" the common name Drusus. If she is correct, this would fit with both the rabbinic materials and these Christian sources as identifying the Jewish use of this name within Mary's family. This would be further evidence that Pantera was a name known and used by first-century Jews even in Jerusalem.

Outside Israel, the name Pantera is found here and there in various sources, with several examples linked to Roman soldiers. One first-century Roman tombstone, noted by Adolf

Deissmann in 1910, has caught the attention of several scholars, including Morton Smith, who wryly suggested it might be the only authentic "relic" of the historical Jesus. It is a tombstone monument of a first-century Roman soldier named Pantera near the Roman camp at Bingerbrück on the Rhine River in Germany. Here is the Latin with an English translation:

Tib. Iul. Abdes. Pantera.
Sidonia. Ann. LXII.
Stipen. XXXX. Miles. Exs.
Coh. I. sagittariorum.
      h. s. e.

Tiberius Julius Abdes Pantera
of Sidon, aged 62
A soldier of 40 years' service,
of the 1st cohort of archers,
      lies here

Tiberius Julius Abdes Pantera was an archer in the Roman army. He was from Sidon, just north of the Upper Galilee on the Mediterranean coast of Syria, only sixty miles from Nazareth, and he served as a Roman soldier for forty years in the first century AD. He apparently received Roman citizenship after twenty-five years of service, taking on the names Tiberius Julius in honor of the emperor Tiberius (14–37 AD), after which he served another fifteen years until his death at age sixty-two. It is possible he might have been Jewish, based on the name Abdes. I have traveled to Germany several times to examine the tombstone and learn what I could about Abdes Pantera and his career. The tombstone is now in the Museum Römerhalle in Bad Kreuznach, not far from the original Roman camp at Bingerbrück. Today there are modern roads and apartments built over the spot. The Roman camp, from what I could tell in consulting with local archaeologists, was nearby on the banks of the Nahe River, which still has foundations of a bridge from Roman times. However, more recent research on the details of Julius Abdes Pantera's career has established that this Pantera was definitely not a soldier at the time Mary would have become pregnant. Whether he was Jewish, and the significance of the names Abdes Pantera, remain uncertain. If Abdes is related to his birthname, Pantera could be descriptive or a nickname or even a moniker, similar to the texts mentioned previously that speak of a "Pantera" in Mary's ancestry.

Some have proposed that Mary might have been raped by a Roman soldier. Their argument is that, given the times in which Mary lived, and especially the unrest in Galilee following the death of Herod the Great, unless Mary willingly violated her engagement, rape is the most likely scenario, with a Roman soldier, perhaps called Pantera, as the perpetrator.

There are several problems with this possibility. First, the earliest ancient source that identifies Pantera as a Roman soldier is the text from Celsus in the late second century, and he says nothing about rape. At the time of the birth of Jesus, which was nearly two years before Herod's death in March of 4 BC, we know of no disturbances in Galilee that would account for women being raped. Roman soldiers were not stationed in Sepphoris or around Nazareth, but in Syria to the north, under the command of Varus. Herod was in firm control of things around the time Jesus was born.

It should also be noted that in the case of this Pantera of Sidon, he would not have to be in the Roman army at the time Mary became pregnant with Jesus. He might well have either joined or been conscripted after Jesus was born, and thus the rumor circulated that Mary had gotten pregnant from a Roman

Tombstone of Pantera, Roman soldier of the first
century, with Latin inscription, Rhine River, Germany

soldier. Since we have sources that claim Pantera was a name
known in the family of Mary, it is entirely possible that Mary
became involved with someone by that name, associated with
her extended family, even before her marriage to Joseph was
arranged by her parents, whether he became a Roman soldier
subsequently or not. Zeichmann, whose work on the inscription is the most thorough, does not think we have any credible
evidence that Abdes Pantera's military unit ever served in the
Sidon area, but then offers this important conclusion:

> This fact alone, however, does not entirely negate the
> prospect of Pantera fathering Jesus, as it is possible
> that he did so before becoming a soldier: Pantera was
> probably of age and still located in the southern Levant
> (i.e., Sidon) around the time Jesus was conceived.

The Gospels report that Jesus traveled to and drew follow-ers from Sidon, which is only sixty miles from Nazareth (Mark 3:8; 7:24–31). He also speaks favorably of the Sidonians as receptive to his message (Luke 10:13). And there seems to be some connection between the Sidonians and the Samaritans that might be relevant. The charge in the Gospels that Jesus was "born of fornication" included the parallel assertion that he was a Samaritan. It is possible that rather than using "Samari-tan" as some general term of abuse, the charge might be much more specific. Josephus tells us that some of the Samaritans claimed they were Sidonians. If there were rumors circulating that Jesus's father was a Samaritan, could that charge include the idea that he had come from Sidon? Remarkably, there are several stories in the life of Jesus that reflect strongly positive attitudes toward Samaritans—the best-known, of course, is the one about the "Good Samaritan," who came to the aid of a Jew left robbed and beaten on the road from Jerusalem to Jericho (Luke 10:29–37). Jesus dealt freely with Samaritans, passing through their territory north of Judea on his way to Galilee. He commended them for their faith and included them in his circle of teaching (Luke 17:11–19)—most notably, the Samaritan woman who was living with a man out of wedlock, having had five previous husbands (John 4:1–42). When Jesus heals ten lepers on the road to Jerusalem from Galilee, sending them off to the priests to be certified as clean, the only one who returns to thank him is a Samaritan (Luke 17:11–19).

Young single women did not routinely mix or socialize with young men, as is still the case to this day in strict religious cultures. Their activities were chaperoned by an older relative. The only opportunity might be in a larger family gathering. So the idea that the name Pantera was one known in Mary's family might make sense.

Women have exercised the right of refusal when it comes to marriage—even if patriarchal societies try to countermand that idea. This drama has generated countless tales worldwide, including the classic case of Tevye's daughter Chava, who falls in love with a Russian villager named Fyedka in *Fiddler on the Roof*. In a great biblical story echoing the same theme, Isaac, the son of Abraham, asks Rebecca's family for her hand in marriage. Rebecca is first asked, "Will you go with this man?" and she answers for herself, "I will go" (Genesis 24:58). It was her willing consent that gave substance to any legal arrangement the parents made for marriage.

We can assume that Mary's parents must have considered Joseph the best match for her, perhaps given his artisan's trade and some degree of social status. Since Joseph disappears from our record after Jesus is age twelve, and we only have references to Jesus's mother and his brothers and sisters, it is likely that he died before his children grew to adulthood. We read that Jesus "went down to Capernaum, with his mother and his brother . . ." (John 2:12). Later he and "his mother and brothers" are living in Peter's house at Capernaum (Mark 3:31). Jesus is called "son of Mary" with his brothers named—James, Joses, Judas, and Simon—and his sisters mentioned (Mark 6:3). And in the final days leading up to Jesus's crucifixion, his mother and siblings are with him (John 19:25; Acts 1:14). It would be strange if Joseph were alive that he never appears a single time in any of our sources past Jesus's childhood. We don't know his age when they married, but one possible explanation of his disappearance is that he was older than Mary. He is described in the Gospel of Matthew as a "just man," who goes ahead with the marriage despite Mary's pregnancy and does not want to bring any shame upon her (Matthew 1:19).

This quest for Mary, ironically, ends up shedding new

insight on the "real" Joseph, who has also been lost to history. Even if he died before Jesus reached adulthood, he was the father of this large family with all the challenges and responsibilities that brings. Clearly, his disappearance—and most likely his early death—had enormous consequences for Mary, raising her children alone, with Jesus likely taking over as head of the house even in his twenties. But we should also remember his life—what little we know of it—which has been lost even to our imagination.

Disagreements over the choice of marriage partners is probably as frequent a source of conflict in families as any other. It is entirely possible that Mary was already involved with Pantera, had become pregnant, and kept it to herself, but when presented with the marriage firmly stood her ground, honoring the child growing within her as a gift of God. Perhaps she believed, in her own way of understanding things, that this special child was "of the Holy Spirit," much like Isaac in the case of Sarah and Abraham (Genesis 18:14; 21:1). In these texts God indeed does "visit" Sarah, who is childless, and as a result she becomes pregnant with Isaac, but through the human agency of Abraham.

It appears likely that she was forced to flee her family to get away from village gossip. According to Luke, immediately after learning about her pregnancy, Mary "arose and went with haste" to the "hill country of Judea," which is a hundred miles south of Nazareth. There she found refuge with her kinswoman Elizabeth, who was pregnant at that time with John the Baptizer (Luke 1:39).

Serapion, a fourth-century bishop from Egypt who writes one of the earliest accounts of the life of John the Baptizer, says that Elizabeth and her husband, Zechariah, who was a priest, lived in Ein Kerem, five miles west of Jerusalem. From

Nazareth, this hundred-mile journey would have taken Mary a minimum of three or four days through some potentially dangerous terrain. Perhaps she was traveling with a trusted servant or friend. On this initial visit, Mary stayed with Elizabeth for three months, probably helping attend to the birth of John, who was six months older than Jesus (Luke 1:36, 56). The two families were clearly very close, and Mary must have considered their household a kind of haven and a second home. Serapion also relates that some years later, when Elizabeth died in the hill country outside Ein Kerem, it was Mary and Jesus's sister Salome who came to assist with her burial, washing her body in the same spring from which they used to draw water.

Jesus's biological father, whoever he might have been, disappears. Whether he was caught up in the massive exile of the Upper Galilee after the 4 BC revolts, or joined the Roman army, or met with any number of other possible fates, we will never know.

No one can possibly know what Mary might have told Jesus about his father, if she chose to relate to her son the circumstances or story of their relationship. Jesus might well have grown up under the stigma of being called "son of Mary," with no father named, as we have seen in our earliest text, the Gospel of Mark. Despite any potential wagging tongues, given her pregnancy, Mary decided to go ahead with her arranged marriage. And if Joseph kept things secret, which may well have been the case, the gossip might have been minimal.

Only Mary knew the full circumstances of her pregnancy. From our end of history we would have to say "father unknown." Mary believed in destiny. Perhaps she raised Jesus with a sense of his specialness, his uniqueness, precisely because she loved and honored his father. If, as we surmise, she was only around fourteen years old, then the entire situation underscores what a remarkable person she was. The identification of Jesus's father remains Mary's secret. I want to honor that secret, and the enduring gifts she gave the world through her life and the lives of her later children with Joseph—as the most influential woman in human history.

Chapter Seven

DOUBLY ROYAL

You are a priest forever according to My word, O
King of Righteousness

—God to David

R ecently, while writing this book, I did "discover" what
I believe to be an ancient document relating to Mary.
Far from hidden in a cave or lost in a monastery for
centuries, it is part of our New Testament—right under our
noses. I refer to the genealogy of Jesus embedded in Luke
3:23–38, which includes a list of forty names from King David
down to Jesus. I am convinced that we have here the lineage
of his mother, not of his legal father, Joseph, found in Matthew, which is completely different (Matthew 1:1–16). The
surprise is, this list contains not only the names of those of the
Davidic lineage, but also priestly names belonging to the line
of Aaron—Israel's first priest—from which sprang the Hasmoneans. Names such as Matthew, Levi, Eliezar, and Jannai
(Janaeus) are priestly, favored by the Hasmoneans. Even one of
Jesus's apostles, Matthew, is also known as Levi—a name associated with the priesthood even down to our own time (Mark
2:14; Luke 5:27). The implications are enormous. Mary has a
dual lineage, from both kings and priests—she is doubly royal.

As are all her children. She had the very thing that Herod and his sons desired the most—and that was the source of Herod Antipas's determination to kill Jesus (Luke 13:31).

The Bible offers dozens of such genealogical records, often referred to as the "begats," whether that of Noah, Abraham, Jacob, or the kings of Israel. Such lists are usually viewed as dry chapters one might skim through or even skip to get back to the real story. But these lineages also provide essential clues about historical succession and legitimacy. I am convinced that this embedded genealogical text is one of our most important sources for recovering the historical Mary. As we have seen with the Herodian family, we are dealing here with matters of life and death, and the singular question of the time—who might legitimately become a ruler of the Jewish people?

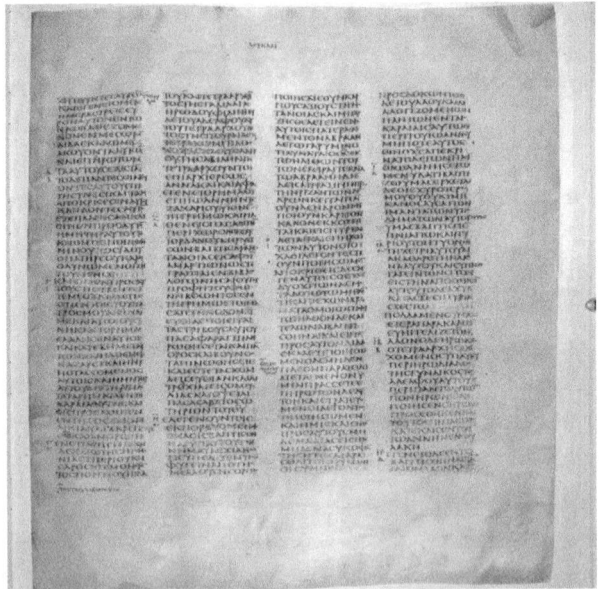

Mary's genealogy in the oldest copy
of the Gospel of Luke

Most scholars who have worked on Luke's genealogy see in it an alternative genealogy of Joseph, unrelated to Mary. This makes no sense, because Matthew's genealogy for Jesus's legal father comes down through King Solomon, son of David. But in Luke the Davidic lineage is traced through Nathan, who was the famous king Solomon's younger brother. We know nothing about this second son beyond his name and that his mother was also Bathsheba (1 Chronicles 3:12). He was fully royal but never assumed the throne. That we would have two very contradictory lineages for Joseph, one in Matthew, the other in Luke, seems highly unlikely. The names in the lists are completely different. The key point is simply to ask who was Joseph's father. He is different in the two lists, as are his grand-father, great-grandfather, back as far as you want to go—until Solomon. If both lists are of Joseph's line, why would Matthew have Joseph's father as Jacob while Luke has Heli (Matthew 1:16; Luke 3:23)? Since these two grandfathers of Jesus are traced from completely different ancestors, they cannot be two names for the same person.

Luke, who provides this alternative genealogy, inserts a qualifying phrase, that clarifies that this is not intended to be Joseph's lineage but that of Mary. An amplified translation would be: Jesus being the son *as was supposed*, of Joseph, *but actually* of Eli (Luke 3:23). Eli is another form of the name for Joachim, father of Mary.

Matthew is giving the *legal* ancestry of Jesus, through Joseph, who took him as his own, whereas Luke provides us with Jesus's biological ancestry through Mary. Many scholars have dis-missed this solution as an attempt to harmonize the Bible by explaining away such obvious contradictions, but there is more going on here. The main argument against this being Mary's lineage is that Jewish records always follow the male lineage, never the female, making it unlikely that Luke is presenting

Mary's biological line. Though commonly repeated, this is not the case.

In Mary's time, such Jewish genealogical records were kept with extraordinary care. They determined all sorts of legal matters involving marriage, property rights, and inheritance. Recall that when Herod drowned Jonathan, the brother of his wife, Mariame, in the swimming pool at Jericho in 35 BC, he was not just eliminating a potential rival who was popular with the people. His broader agenda was to eradicate the distinguished Hasmonean line of high priests who had ruled an independent Jewish state since the victory of the Maccabees over the Greeks in 164 BC. Herod's execution of Hyrcanus, Jonathan's grandfather, in 31 BC, at the advanced age of eighty, despite his mutilated ears already disqualifying him from serving as a priest, was to the same end. Why else kill an old man who posed no threat to him?

It all had to do with priestly or kingly pedigree, and Herod lacked both.

This was Herod's first order of business as soon as he consolidated his relationship with Octavian—soon to be the emperor Augustus. Herod feared that Hyrcanus, even with his mutilated ears, might plot to restore other surviving members of that priestly lineage to office. Hyrcanus had sided with the Parthians and Antigonus, Herod's great rival, during the conflict that ended with Herod becoming king of Judea in AD 30. Herod never forgave that, despite Mariame's pleas to spare the old man. According to Josephus, once Jonathan was removed, Herod appointed undeserving men *without pedigree* as high priests in his place, virtually eliminating the traditional line of hereditary priests that had passed from father to son for several centuries, turning the priesthood into a political appointment by his command.

Herod's own ancestry was plagued with questions of legitimacy, including the gossip that his father, Antipater, was in fact the son of a temple slave or prostitute in the city of Ashkelon. This story, preserved by Julius Africanus, a late-second-century Christian writer and a native of Jerusalem, asserts that Idumean brigands attacked Ashkelon and took away Antipater, who had himself been a temple slave. Antipater was, accordingly, brought up as an Idumean. Since the Idumeans had converted to Judaism under John Hyrcanus, Antipater considered himself a Jew, rising in wealth and influence. Antipater wisely sided with Julius Caesar in his defeat of Pompey, and Caesar granted him Roman citizenship and appointed him the first Roman procurator over Judea. His task was to pacify the countryside and clear out various rebels and upstarts. As we have seen, Antipater appointed his son Herod governor over Galilee in 47 BC, and it was his defeat of the Jewish "messiah" Hezekiah that established a foothold for this foreign Idumean family as the undisputed rulers of the land. Whether true or not, rumors take on a life of their own, and Herod was determined to extinguish this one (much like Adolf Hitler tried to stamp out gossip that he was the illegitimate child of a Jewish employer of his mother). Africanus claims to have found this story in various histories of the Greeks.

This slander, coupled with charges that he was a foreigner, a commoner, and a half-Jew, only fueled Herod's ambition and drove him to take a particularly drastic action. Julius Africanus, an early-third-century Christian historian known for his carefully researched chronicles, says that Herod ordered the burning of all public genealogical records to ensure that none of the leading Jewish families could prove an ancestry nobler than his. We know that some of these records, especially for those who lived in Galilee, were kept at Sepphoris. Josephus tells us that in his own day Sepphoris was the seat of the royal bank and the archives. We also have references in rabbinic literature to "the ancient archives in Sepphoris." This comes from a much later time—well into the second or third century—but the prominence of Sepphoris as the urban center of Galilee goes back to Mary's lifetime. Africanus wrote:

> Now a few who were careful, having private records for themselves, either remembering the names or otherwise deriving them from copies, gloried in the preservation of the memory of their good birth; among these were those mentioned above, called *desposuni*, because of their relation to the family of the Savior, and from the Jewish villages of Nazareth and Cochaba they traversed the rest of the land and expounded the preceding genealogy of their descent.

This is a remarkable bit of evidence. Despite Herod's desperate actions, various families kept their own private records. In the case of Mary, we have *specific* references to members of her family who were from the Nazareth area, later called *desposuni*, literally "kinsmen of the Lord," preserving these precious records with great care. Richard Bauckham has persuasively argued that the author of Luke had access to these records, preserved by the first generation of Jesus's family, and that he passed them on in essentially the same form as he received them, embedding them in his Gospel: "The Lukan genealogy of Jesus is a more important historical document than has been generally appreciated. I am convinced that it comes down to us in virtually the form that Luke has preserved from the circle of the first generation of the *desposynoi*." Although Bauckham is not convinced this is the genealogy of Mary, that possibility changes everything. It would mean we have access to a precious original document,

King David	Joshua	Mattathias
Nathan	Er	Naggai
Mattatha	Elmadam	Hesli
Menna	Cosam	Naham
Melea	Addi	Amos
Eliakim	Melchi	Mattathias
Jonam	Neri	Joseph
Joseph	Shealtiel	Jannai
Judah	Zerubbabel	Melchi
Simeon	Rhesa	Levi
Levi	Joanan	Matthat
Matthat	Joda	Heli or Eli
Jorim	Josech	Mary
Eliezar	Sem	Jesus

Mary's mixed royal and priestly lineage from chapter 3 of Luke

hitherto unrecognized, related to Mary's distinguished ancestry. For a historian who has worked on these materials for decades, the idea is breathtaking, akin to finding a lost manuscript in a cave in the desert.

Paul never mentions Mary by name, although he undoubtedly met her on his visits to Jerusalem when he conferred with Jesus's brother James and other apostles, such as Peter and John (Galatians 1:19; 2:9; Acts 15:12–21). But notice that he says clearly that Jesus "was descended from David, according to the flesh" (Romans 1:4). Paul is our earliest evidence of that affirmation—but when he refers to his parentage, he simply says Jesus is "born of a woman," with no reference to his father. Since he is not focused on Jesus "according to the flesh," it is of no consequence to him—but he knows it qualifies him to be called the Davidic Messiah.

It is here, with Paul, that we see the beginning of a process of blotting out Mary's life. It is conscious and deliberate, intended to shift Jesus and his revolutionary significance from earth to heaven, and thus away from the Jewish mother who helped to shape him.

The reigns of Herod the Great and his son Herod Antipas were far removed from these later attempts to spiritualize political realities in favor of a heavenly kingdom beyond this world. Mary's unique pedigree put her and her children at risk in a time when dozens of messiahs of all sorts and descriptions were regularly being beheaded or crucified by the Romans.

To be a legitimate priest, one's direct lineage had to be traced back to Aaron—Moses's brother—who was of the tribe of Levi (Exodus 28:1; 29:44). Similarly, only those of the direct lineage of King David could be considered royals—potentially sitting on David's throne. Neither the Persians nor the Greeks nor the Romans allowed the Jews to have a native Jewish king of the line of David, knowing this would stir up national longings for independence and dreams of the messianic age. Given this lack of a Davidic king, the Hasmonean high priests began increasingly to take on "royal" airs. Josephus says that John Hyrcanus, as revered as he was, combined into his single office the three "most desirable" things: ruler of the nation, the high priesthood, and the gift of prophecy. Yet he still did not dare take the title of king, knowing that was reserved for the coming Davidic Messiah.

When John Hyrcanus died, everything changed. His ambitious eldest son, Aristobulus, put his mother and his four brothers in prison, starving his mother to death. He was the first to put a diadem on his head, daring to use the title of king formally on his coins. The Pharisees, the dominant religious party of the time, were furious, knowing this title could rightly be given only to a descendant of King David. Aristobulus's reign lasted just a year. He was in poor health and died from internal bleeding, possibly caused by poisoning. He was succeeded by his powerful wife, Salome Alexandra, who released his brothers from prison and married the eldest, Alexander Jannaeus.

What most distinguished Jannaeus's long rule was that he began to emphasize his role as king even over that of priest. The ancient Greek geographer and chronicler Strabo records that "Alexander Jannaeus was the first to declare himself king instead of priest." This reference from a non-Jewish writer is telling. We would not expect Strabo to know of the one-year reign of Aristobulus, but it is notable that Jannaeus's bold move was recorded by a Greek historian.

Remarkably, Jannaeus's coins illustrate this process of usurping the kingship. They fall into two major types: royal and priestly. The royal coins are mostly bilingual—Hebrew and Greek—and are characterized by the Paleo-Hebrew inscription "Yehonatan the King" along with the lily emblem—which in English is "Jonathan the King." The other side of the coin shows the symbol of the anchor along with the Greek inscription "of King Alexander." This anchor symbol was minted by his father, John Hyrcanus, who had not dared to put "the king" on any of his coins. What stands out is that Jannaeus "overstruck" his coins at some point in his reign, inserting his claim to be king on previous mintages that had only made him "Head of the Council of the Jews."

Jannaeus coin inscribed
"King Alexander"

Jannaeus was a horrible despot. He is called a "furious young Lion" in the Dead Sea Scrolls, "who filled his cave with a mass of corpses . . . hanging men alive." We know from Josephus that this is a reference to his mass crucifixion of eight hundred Pharisees who opposed his rule. He celebrated the slaughter by feasting with his concubines in the sight of the whole city—most likely on the Mount of Olives—and ordering the throats of the women and children of the men crucified to be cut before their eyes while they were still alive. On another occasion, at the Festival of Tabernacles, people began to pelt him with the citrons that are part of the palm-branch ceremony of the season, and he had six thousand of them slain in retaliation.

At Jannaeus's death in 76 BC, his wife, Salome Alexandra, ruled as "queen of the Jews" for nearly ten years. While she has often been called the "forgotten Jewish queen," she is one of only seven historically known persons mentioned by name in the Dead Sea Scrolls, and the only woman. Her Hebrew name was Shlomzion, which means "peace of Zion," and in both Hebrew and Greek became one of the most popular women's names for the next hundred years. One of Queen Salome's first acts was to make peace with the Pharisees. She is remembered as a nobler ruler than either of her despotic husbands, and she established precedent for a woman to reign as queen without the formal designation of king or priest, since as a woman she was not allowed to hold either title. However, she was the last ruler to preside over an independent Jewish state, as the Roman general Pompey invaded and put the entire country under Roman rule in 63 BC. Salome's two sons, Aristobulus and Hyrcanus, became bitter rivals for the priesthood. According to Josephus, Salome died mysteriously of a "serious illness" much before her time, resulting in the political rivalry for power that would be resolved only by the Romans appointing Herod king of the Jews.

Salome was the grandmother of Antigonus, Herod's archrival. Like his grandfather, he overtly claimed to be "king of the Jews," backed up by Parthian military support, though he was a priest and lacked any Davidic ancestry. We have already seen how Herod defeated him and had him crucified and beheaded.

What this means is that during the lifetimes of Joachim, Anna, and Mary, the line between priest and king was being increasingly blurred—and their family legitimately had *both*, so they were doubly royal. The most common objection to this idea of Mary passing on this rare lineage to her children is that she would need to be a man. But such categories are never airtight, and they are often contradicted in practice. Few realize that in ancient Israel there was a queen—Athaliah, who ruled for seven years (2 Kings 8:26; 2 Chronicles 22:2). Mary's place as matriarch of the Jesus movement—or, as it were, queen mother of the Messiah in the Nazarene community—opened the way for an alternative interpretation. We even have David's sons called priests, and David himself wore the priestly ephod, the ceremonial linen garment, and was allowed to enter the holy place of the Ark of the Covenant in procession with the priests (2 Samuel 8:18, 6:14; I Chronicles 15:27). It is only a dominant male patriarchy that would claim *women* of David's line could not pass on the right of their Davidic lineage. In the Second Temple period (520 BC to AD 70), traditional territorial affiliations with this or that tribe, as allotted in the Torah, became irrelevant. Jews of any tribal identity could live anywhere in the land—and there were more Jews outside the land of Israel, scattered all over the Roman world, than inside, with lots of intermarriage.

Potentially, this mobility could allow a woman to carry her tribal affiliation or status into a marriage and thus pass it on to her children. We have seen that Herod the Great thought his marriage to Mariame might carry with it a degree of affiliation with the lineage of the Hasmoneans, imparting such status to his children.

Later, in Mary's time, Herod's son Antipas, whose mother,

Malthace, was a Samaritan, had the same idea. He divorced his Nabatean Arab wife to marry the beautiful Jewish princess Herodias, who was already married to his half brother Herod Philip. While Antipas was enticed by Herodias's legendary beauty, clearly his main motive was to bolster his lack of pedigree through such a union. Herodias was the daughter of Aristobulus, one of the two sons of Mariame from Herod the Great himself. Antipas must have thought it would mitigate his own Samaritan pedigree to marry the granddaughter of Herod and Mariame. This gives the phrase "all in the family" a new meaning! This is the same Herodias whose daughter Salome demanded John the Baptizer's head be brought into the banquet hall on a platter at the urging of her mother. John had condemned her relationship with Herod as adulterous. She may well also have been involved in urging Herod to do away with Jesus as well—in his eyes Jesus was like a reincarnation of John (Mark 6:14; Luke 13:31). She and her husband Antipas lived in Sepphoris in a luxurious palace during the very years Jesus was growing up. Jesus once referred to those "gorgeously appareled who live in luxury in king's courts," a direct reference to Herod Antipas and his wife (Luke 6:25).

There are passages in the Torah indicating that the term "offspring" (the Hebrew *zerah,* meaning "seed") does not refer exclusively to men, but to women as well. The foundational text takes us back to the Garden of Eden, where the serpent is told: "And I will put enmity between you and the woman, and between your seed and her seed; he shall bruise your head, and you shall bruise his heel" (Genesis 3:15). Here it is the "seed" of the woman that gives rise to humanity. A bit earlier in the narrative, when Eve is created, it reads: "The man called his wife's name Eve because she was the mother of all living" (Genesis 3:20). Later in the Torah, in speaking of childbirth: "If a woman conceives [literally, 'seeds seed'], and bears a male child, then she shall be unclean seven days; as at the time of her menstruation, she shall be unclean" (Leviticus 12:2). It also says in the New Testament that Sarah, the aged wife of Abraham who had no children, was "given the power to conceive," but the Greek text literally says she "received the ability to produce seed [*spermatos*]" (Hebrews 13:11). In Hebrew culture a child is born of the "seed" of both the mother and the father.

Hippolytus of Rome is one of our most important Christian writers of the late second and early third centuries. He refers several times in his writings to Jesus's mixed ancestry, combining both the tribe of Judah and the tribe of Levi, giving him an ancestral right to serve as both priest and king. He writes that Jesus was "tribally mixed," descending from David as well as the priestly lineage of Aaron. Irenaeus and Origen, two of our most authoritative and influential early Christian writers, make the same observation. Luke tells us that Mary is a "kinswoman" of Elizabeth, the mother of John the Baptizer, who is a daughter of Aaron, married to the priest Zechariah (Luke 1:5). The Greek word *suggenis*—"kinswoman"—refers to a close relative, most likely an aunt, in this case perhaps the sister of Mary's mother, Anna.

This notion of Jesus—and thus of Mary—being "tribally mixed" was firmly established in some of our earliest Christian sources. Hegesippus, a second-century Jewish convert to Christianity, reports that Mary's second-born son, James, who was appointed head of the Christian community after the death of Jesus, wore the prescribed linen garment of a priest, never wool (Exodus 44:17). In the first century, before the term "Christian" was used, the Jesus movement was commonly known as the Nazarenes (Acts 24:5; 11:26). According to Epiphanius, another early Christian writer, who cites earlier sources, James served as "high priest" for the Nazarene community, wearing the priestly diadem on his head and entering the holy precincts of the Jerusalem temple reserved only for those who were priests. These remarkable assertions show that James was viewed as having inherited a priestly pedigree from his mother, Mary. This also shows that later attempts to claim that James and the other brothers of Jesus were children of Joseph by a previous marriage are invalid, since Joseph had no claim whatsoever to any priestly status, judging from the very different lineage that Matthew preserved.

There is also a remarkable Greek text titled "On the Priesthood of Jesus," dating from the reign of the emperor Justinian in the sixth century. It relates that Mary provided the priests in Jerusalem, who had questioned Jesus's right to claim the priesthood, with the genealogical proof that she carried the mixed lineage of Judah and Levi. Although the text itself is late and legendary, it is a further witness to this idea, passed down over the centuries within the Christian tradition in a wide variety of sources, that Jesus carried this mixed tribal ancestry—as did James and his other brothers.

We know the most about James, who took over leadership of the church until he was brutally murdered in AD 63 by the high priest Annas in Jerusalem. He is mentioned in many of our sources—in the New Testament, by various early Christian writers, and even in Gnostic Christian texts. He is usually called "the brother of the Lord" without any qualification. We even have one text, discovered in Egypt in 1945, called the Second Apocalypse of James, in which Mary says to Jesus and James, "Both of you were nourished with the same milk." Joses is a nickname for Joseph—the second brother—much like Jim for James in English; Judas and Simon, the two younger brothers, are listed in reverse order, as Simon and Judas, in Matthew's parallel account (Matthew 13:55). It is likely that Mark lists the birth order—certainly Jesus was the eldest and James next in line. Judas, not to be confused with Judas Iscariot, who betrayed Jesus, is the author of the New Testament Epistle of Jude and calls himself the "brother of James" (Jude 1).

Israeli historian Tal Ilan is the undisputed expert on ancient Jewish names in this period. Her monumental work, dealing with naming conventions in the land of Israel in the time of Mary has definitively demonstrated that when males are referred to as "son of" their mother rather than their father, it can reflect a recognition of pedigree—particularly in the case of a priestly or royal lineage. That means when Jesus is identified as "son of Mary" it can indicate that Joseph is not the father, but also that Mary is "highborn" and thus doubly royal.

Mark is the earliest witness to Mary and her extended family. Instead of the story of Mary bearing the single child Jesus without sexual intercourse and remaining a virgin her entire life, Mark allows us to open our minds to reconsider a completely different, but more historical narrative: Mary as the single widowed mother of this large family, singlehandedly raising them through one of the most troubled and trying times in Jewish history. It is rather striking that Mark, the earliest Gospel, says nothing about Joseph whatsoever—he is neither named nor even referenced as "father" anywhere in the entire Gospel, in contrast to our three later Gospels. Mark is the only one who dares to call Jesus "son of Mary," and yet he clearly believes that Jesus is of the "house of David." I am convinced that this expression primarily indicates Mary's singular importance as the doubly royal mother of this extraordinary messianic family.

The implications of this mixed priestly and royal lineage for Mary are weighty. This means Jesus and the rest of her children shared this doubly royal ancestry, and three of them ended up murdered because of it: Jesus, James, and Simon. Herod the Great, his sons who ruled as his successors, and the entire line of Hasmonean priestly rulers longed for this sort of pedigree. Augustus could declare Herod "king of the Jews," and the

Hasmoneans tried desperately to be viewed as kings in the eyes of the people, yet they lacked the ancestry. But Mary and her children had both. We must remember that the events in our Gospels were not "done in a corner," as the saying goes. This special family was on the radar of Herod Antipas, who had John the Baptizer murdered and who sought to kill Jesus. Both posed the same threat—which Josephus makes explicit—a fear that they could raise a popular uprising with their claims of royal and priestly pedigrees through their mothers, Mary and Elizabeth. And on the priestly side of things, the family of the high priest Annas was instrumental in having both Jesus and his brother James murdered as well.

In Mark, Jesus puts a final startling question to his enemies in the temple in Jerusalem two days before his death: How is it that the Messiah is a son of David when David calls this future ruler his "Lord," addressing him directly: "You are a priest forever, according to my word, O righteous king" (Mark 12:35–37; Psalm 110:1–4). They were completely stumped, and gave no reply—since the idea that the Davidic Messiah would be both a king and a priest was not part of their expectations.

Having delved now into the birth of Mary, her messianic pedigree, and the turbulent times in which she lived, what can be said about her life and her remarkable role as matriarch of the movement Jesus inaugurated?

Chapter Eight

MARY IN JERUSALEM

And Mary, the mother of Jesus, was there, with his
brothers and the women.

      —Acts of the Apostles

During the past three decades I have participated in
a half-dozen licensed archaeological excavations that
relate directly to my quest for the historical Mary.
These include digging in Jerusalem on Mount Zion, where
Mary spent the last years of her life; excavating at Sepphoris,
near Nazareth, where Mary was born and grew up; exploring a
cave near Ein Kerem, outside Jerusalem, the home of the family
of John the Baptizer, who was closely related to her; excavating caves at Qumran in the Judean desert, where the Dead Sea
Scrolls were discovered; and exploring a cave tomb in Jerusalem
that might be associated with Mary's burial.

When I am excavating in Jerusalem, I always stay in the Old
City, in the Christian Quarter with its Latin and Greek patri-
archates. I know the winding streets and alleyways intimately.
The names of these streets are quite telling: St. Peter, St. Paul,
and even St. Francis and St. Helena—the emperor Constantine's mother—are all represented. James, son of Mary and
brother of Jesus, is nowhere to be found. For that you must go

to the Armenian Quarter, just to the south, on Mount Zion—the oldest Christian community of Jerusalem. There one finds St. James Cathedral, as well as a side street leading to the Jewish Quarter also named St. James. The Armenian tradition has preserved much about James, as well as his mother, Mary, and the importance of Mount Zion to Jesus's followers after his death.

For more than a decade my focus has been on the southwestern hill of ancient Jerusalem, today known as Mount Zion. Mary's presence there is inescapable, not only twelve to fifteen feet below the present ground level, but in the foundations of the ancient structures and holy places still visited each year by millions of Christian pilgrims.

St. James Street in the Armenian Quarter
of Jerusalem, Mount Zion

Many later-ninth-century traditions place Mary with the apostle John, the Galilean fisherman, living out her last days in Selçuk, Turkey, near ancient Ephesus. This site, where visitors are shown a "house of the Virgin Mary," draws a million tourists a year. Popes Paul VI and John Paul II have celebrated Mass there. But this Ephesus site has no credible historical backing, despite its current popularity. Its recent discovery is based on the visions of the early-nineteenth-century nun Anne Catherine Emmerich. It depends on a related idea, accepted by many Christians as dogma, that the unnamed "disciple whom Jesus loved," mentioned in four scenes in the Gospel of John, was the apostle John, one of the twelve, who is said to have spent his last days in Ephesus.

Both ideas are mistaken.

There is no historical evidence that puts John the apostle in Asia, and it is most unlikely that he is this mysterious Beloved Disciple, despite the popular, near universal assumption. Traditions, even with no historical basis whatsoever, often die a hard death. The John who lived in Asia is another John, most often referred to as John the Elder. What we have here is a classic case of mistaken identity.

There is, however, persuasive evidence that the "disciple whom Jesus loved" is none other than Jesus's brother James, Mary's second-born son. This mysterious unnamed disciple is mentioned only four times in the Gospel of John. He suddenly appears at the Last Supper, affectionately leaning against Jesus as they reclined for the evening meal (John 13:23–25). He is then with Mary, mother of Jesus, along with Mary Magdalene and other women, standing before the cross at the crucifixion of Jesus, who speaks to Mary and to him with the famous words "Mother, behold your son. Son, behold your mother"—and we are told that from that hour this unnamed disciple "took her into his own home" (John 19:26–27). Next, he shows up at Jesus's tomb—right after Mary Magdalene had visited before sunrise and discovered that Jesus's body was gone (John 20:2–8). Finally, he is on the shores of the Sea of Galilee after the group came to believe Jesus was raised up from the dead (21:1–24). This unnamed figure cannot be one of the twelve, since all of them forsook Jesus and fled when he was arrested, and

Peter even denied knowing him three times during Jesus's trial before the high priests. It is quite inconceivable, despite the later Christian identification of this disciple with John, that Jesus would bypass his brother James, the next-oldest, who by all rights in Jewish tradition would care for his own mother.

All our textual sources, both in the New Testament and in texts of the earliest church historians, are unambiguously clear that James the brother of Jesus, who became known as James the Just, the second-born son of Mary, took over as leader of the movement when Jesus died.

This later-second-century tradition that John the son of Zebedee, the fisherman from Galilee, took charge of Mary after Jesus's death is a weak attempt to *write James out of the story*—since by that time the perpetual virginity of Mary was beginning to take hold, and it was denied that she ever had children other than Jesus. And yet the editors of the Gospel of John know full well that Jesus would not just leave his mother abandoned—so they reluctantly introduced James as the one who stepped in to care for her by adopting these mysterious references to a "disciple whom Jesus loved" without giving his name. We can further eliminate John the fisherman as a candidate for this unnamed disciple, since he was one of the twelve. All of our Gospels report that these disciples fled away at Jesus's arrest in the Garden of Gethsemane, with Judas betraying him and Peter following clandestinely at a distance. Further, the Gospel of John mentions the "sons of Zebedee," the fishermen brothers James and John, meeting Jesus at the Sea of Galilee after his resurrection. They are distinguished from this mysterious "disciple whom Jesus loved," who is never named or identified (John 21:1–2, 20).

Remarkably, this inclusion of James escapes censorship in another gospel that survives only in scattered fragments—the Gospel of the Hebrews. It is preserved in quotations from

Jerome, the fifth-century Christian theologian. There we read the following account:

> When the Lord had given the linen cloth to the servant of the priest, he went to James and appeared to him. For James had sworn that he would not eat bread from that hour in which he had drunk the cup of the Lord until he should see him risen from among them that sleep. And shortly thereafter the Lord said: Bring a table and bread! And immediately it is added: he took the bread, blessed it and brake it and gave it to James the Just and said to him: My brother, eat thy bread, for the Son of man is risen from among them that sleep.

Since we don't have any context preserved, we are not sure what role this linen cloth played or who the servant of the priest might have been, but this remarkable text tells us a lot. James is referred to by his honorific title, James the Just, which is never used in the New Testament but is quite common in other, later sources. Second, James was present at the Last Supper, which would otherwise have excluded him as a candidate for being the elusive "disciple whom Jesus loved" who leans against Jesus's breast during the dinner.

Most significant is that Paul knows of this encounter—when he lists those to whom Jesus appeared after his resurrection, he passes on the tradition that "he appeared to James" (I Corinthians 15:7). Yet this encounter is never related in any of our New Testament Gospels.

Mark, our earliest Gospel, followed by Matthew and Luke—all of whom recount the scene of the Last Supper—either does not know or chooses not to say that James is present, possibly because he wants to favor Paul as the main successor of Jesus, rather than James, the leader of the Jerusalem church.

The second-century Coptic Gospel of Thomas, referenced earlier regarding rumors of Jesus's illegitimacy, has a saying that jumps off the page: "The disciples say to Jesus, 'We know you will leave us. Who is going to be our leader then?' Jesus said to them, 'No matter where you go you are to go to James the Just, for whose sake heaven and earth came into being'" (Saying 12).

This dynastic succession of leadership up through the end of the first century is well documented in our sources, with James taking the "throne" or "seat" of Jesus as leader of the movement. James, and his brothers Simon and Judas and others of Mary's extended family, were primary members of the *desposuni*—"kinsmen of the Lord," as noted previously. They succeeded one another as a kind of "council of twelve" over the Jerusalem group both before and after the destruction of Jerusalem. Eusebius lists fifteen by name, including Simon, the brother of James and Jude. When Hadrian became emperor, and the disastrous second Jewish revolt broke out around AD 132, the group was scattered, and Hadrian sought out and killed any families that could claim Davidic lineage, much like Vespasian and his son Domitian had done before him.

Paul, who met and knew James face-to-face, identifies him as the clear leader of the Jesus movement following the crucifixion, ahead of even Peter and John. Paul calls these three the "pillars of the church," but ranks James ahead of the others (Galatians 1:19; 2:9). In later sources James gets the added description of "the Just," to distinguish him from the two apostles named James who were part of the twelve. It was from James the Just, not Peter or Paul, as later tradition has it, that the apostles and disciples sought direction. The reason few know much of anything about Jesus's brother James is because his leadership role was almost completely erased from later church tradition, while denying even the existence of his other siblings. A primary avenue in recovering the lost Mary involves understanding the towering leadership role of James, who led the Jesus movement for over thirty years from Jerusalem with Mary at his side, along with his other brothers and sisters and the apostles Jesus had chosen.

Original foundation stones of the Church
of the Apostles on Mount Zion

It was there, on Mount Zion, that Mary lived in the decades following the crucifixion of Jesus with her oldest living son, James, and his family, and perhaps any of Jesus's unmarried sisters. This is the same house where Jesus ate his last meal with his disciples in the "upper room" (Mark 14:13–17). They regathered there in that same "upper room" at the festival of Pentecost, seven weeks after the crucifixion, where we are told that "Mary was there with his brothers," apparently the leader of a band of women who had come from Galilee (Acts 1:14). This family headquarters for the movement, presumably made available by the unnamed owner of the house, is directly referenced again later in the book of Acts. During his short reign (41–44) Herod Agrippa, grandson of Herod the Great, had beheaded James the son of Zebedee, brother of John, and then arrested Peter, planning to kill him as well. When Peter was able to escape from prison, he went to the house of Mark, where many followers had gathered in hiding, shocked by these events. Peter went into hiding but told the group to "go tell James and the brothers" that he was safe (Acts 12:17). Paul mentions that he went to Jerusalem to meet "James the Lord's brother," three years after his dramatic Damascus visionary experience of "seeing" Jesus—which would have been around AD 38 (Galatians 1:18–19). Then, around AD 50, the book of Acts mentions another crucial gathering hosted by James the brother of Jesus—at which Peter and Paul were present, presumably in the same space (Acts 15). Mary is never mentioned in these many references, but she was very much the matriarch of this large and bustling household, which likely included her sister as well as various women from Galilee, among them Mary Magdalene, who had also moved to Jerusalem (Acts 1:14; John 19:25; Luke 23:49, 24:10).

In the first century AD this area was completely inside the walls of the ancient city. Its courtyard houses were destroyed in AD 70, when the entire city, with the magnificent Jewish temple, went up in flames, brutally sacked by the Romans in response to the Jewish revolt of 66–73. James, and presumably Mary, were dead by that time; but the followers of Jesus, including some of his other family members, led by his brother Simon—who had replaced James in AD 62—returned to Jerusalem around AD 75. They rebuilt this house, making use of the foundation levels of the original building and courtyard, turning it into a synagogue—which Christians subsequently called the Church of the Apostles. In the letter of James to the entire movement, he refers to the meeting place of the movement as a "synagogue," not a church (James 2:1–2). The two terms mean about the same thing in Greek—an assembly or gathering place. Church is *ekklesia* and synagogue is *synagoge*—but once Christians parted ways with their Jewish culture, they became quite distinct. Christian pilgrims flock to this site today, known as the Upper Room or Cenacle. There are few tours that do not include it. What many might not realize is that the present two-thousand-square-foot structure they visit only dates back to Crusader times. In May 2014, Pope Francis held a historic Mass there, delivering a sermon that was broadcast to the world in which he noted the history of that space as it related to Mary and the apostles.

It is what lies underneath that begins to tell us a forgotten story. Archaeologists recently exposed its foundations in new excavations and research. The results that are emerging allow us a glimpse at the history of this area of Jerusalem. We can now locate the foundational walls and courtyard of this first-century house, giving us an idea of its basic dimensions. Given what we have learned from the excavations of other wealthy first-century homes nearby, including the current "priestly mansion" that my colleagues and I are excavating on Mount Zion just to the east of the Cenacle, we have a good idea of what the ground floor, upper, and roof levels of such a courtyard house looked like. Below the ground floor were often chambers that included the kitchen for food preparation, storage rooms, cisterns, a *mikvah* for ritual purity, and sometimes even a bath. The ground level opened onto the walled courtyard, with a fire pit and bread oven. It was the busiest part of the house during the day, with all the bustle of family activities, servants, visitors, and household business carried out in the open space. Just inside the main first-floor entrance was a large reception room with furniture and seating areas, with various smaller adjoining rooms for domestic activities, sleeping, and storage. The upper room was large enough for groups to gather for meetings or business, with adjacent rooms for storage or sleeping. The roof was flat with a wall around and the family would sleep outdoors much of the year, weather permitting, and meals were also eaten there.

The view from Mount Zion was spectacular, as it was the highest peak of the city—with Jerusalem itself twenty-four hundred feet above sea level, and the first-century house that Mary and her family lived in is at the summit. Even today, on the roof of the Cenacle, one can easily imagine the view in Mary's time. You would have seen the entire lower city to the east and north, as well as Herod's magnificent temple with its courtyards and porches in the distance. Sunrise over the Mount of Olives is spectacular, as the rays first peek over the summit; and sunsets are equally glorious, looking to the west. The entire city was built of a pinkish Jerusalem limestone, as it is today, and it took on the colors of the sunlight depending on the time of day.

Mary, as the matriarch of the group, would have had the responsibility of handling the day-to-day operation of this important "headquarters" household. As the movement began to grow rapidly, and spread abroad, this house of James and Mary became the nerve center of the entire Jesus movement worldwide, with traveling visitors and overnight guests and a myriad of activities and meetings. As the mother of Jesus *and* James, her central position was clear.

The reason the foundations and outline of the original first-century house are still preserved is that its rebuilding around AD 75 incorporated some of the foundational stones of the original building. In the 1950s, plaster from the original floor was discovered about two feet below the current surface, along with graffiti left by later pilgrims, reading "Conquer, Savior, Mercy" and "O Jesus that I may live." One of our earliest records is the visit by the Bordeaux pilgrim in AD 333, whose firsthand itinerary has survived and who reports he entered Mount Zion and the "synagogue" was still visible. In the Byzantine period the Hagia Zion church was built next to it, and considered the second-holiest site in Christendom—second only to the Church of the Holy Sepulchre. When that was burned by the Persians in the seventh century, the magnificent Crusader church of St. Mary of Mount Zion incorporated the walls of the restored structure as part of the basilica itself, and the Crusader Upper Room, or Cenacle, is what pilgrims visit today.

Ironically, in all of Jerusalem, this Crusader structure is the only site that is visited simultaneously by both Jewish and Christian pilgrims and tourists, crammed together as their respective guides vie to be heard over the clamor. The Christians visit the second-story Upper Room, while the Jews pray in the lower ground-floor level that they believe is the tomb of King David. Where there are crowds, there are vendors, with their stands set up by early morning, selling freshly baked bread, roasted nuts, ice cream, and drinks, their voices trumpeting their wares over the general din.

The courtyard area, still with the covered remains of the first-century cistern that provided water for the household, is one of the most sacred places in Jerusalem. Our Mount Zion excavation is just a three-minute walk away. We arrive to excavate as the eastern sky is beginning to show some light, and I have often walked to the courtyard in the early morning when it is silent and deserted, just as the roosters are beginning to crow around the city. I sit on the concrete cover of the cistern and try to imagine Mary living out her years in that very space.

Glassed-in statue of Mary in Jerusalem's
Old City along Latin Patriarchate Street

Mary's presence is still palpable throughout the Christian areas of the Old City of Jerusalem. As one walks through the Latin, Greek, Syriac, or Armenian areas, she is everywhere, in the names of shops, churches, and guest houses, and depicted in paintings, statues, wooden carvings, ceramics, necklaces, rosaries, pendants, and holy cards.

On St. Peter's Street, a stone's throw away from where I usually stay in the Old City, one sees a lifelike statue of a young Mary enclosed in a glass case on a pedestal. She wears a scarlet robe with a gold-trimmed green mantle. Often, passing that spot, I stop and gaze into her eyes. I want to talk to her, to let her out of the case and allow her to walk the streets of Jerusalem again. What would she think of the devotion she receives from the millions of tourists who stream through the Old City? She would know nothing of Christianity or the churches or cathedrals in which she is revered and remembered, or the statues, hymns, creeds, and liturgies testifying to her memory. And yet, because of the later theological idea that she was the perpetual Virgin who brought Christ into the world, she was given a central place in Christianity—not for what she was in her own time, but as a cornerstone of Marian theology.

As a Jewish woman Mary would be much more at home in the Jewish Quarter of the city, with its rhythms of Sabbaths, Jewish holy day festivals, and the strains of the Hebrew prayers and liturgical songs intoned at the Western Wall. That realization has inspired my wish to bring her home so she can be seen again as she was in her own time and place, honoring her as "first founder" of the entire Jesus movement, even reaching back to the birth of John the Baptizer.

Chapter Nine

How Mary Was Lost

Nothing is covered up that will not be revealed, or
hidden that will not be known.

—Jesus

The historical Mary I have sought to recover in this
book was marginalized, erased, and betrayed in a process that unfolded over the centuries. It was not systematic, nor was it orchestrated. No witnesses ever appeared to
protest any single obvious stage of this process. No supporters
arrayed on the opposing lines to speak on Mary's behalf. Her
effacement and erasure were part of a complex confluence of
theological, cultural, and political forces that shaped her into
the Blessed Ever-Virgin Mother of God—the most notable
woman in human history—while the real Mary was completely
lost.

Her marginalization isn't unlike that of many other women
whose stories and lives have been lost to history. As the mother
of Jesus, she was not so much forgotten as sidelined. The problem at this earliest stage had nothing to do with preserving
her virginity—that came much later. She and Joseph lived as
a normal Jewish married couple with children; that much is

freely acknowledged, even in Matthew, who speaks of Joseph "knowing his wife" after the birth of Jesus (Matthew 1:25).

In the New Testament Mary and her family are simply dropped from the story, other than what little we can piece together about James. We must never forget that we are talking here about a doubly royal family descended from the hidden lineage of King David, one that surprisingly came to the attention of Herod Antipas and the emperors of Rome. The early Christian historian Eusebius reports that the emperor Vespasian, following the Jewish revolt of AD 66–73, "ordered a search be made for all who were of the family of David, that there might be left among the Jews no one of the royal family."

This blotting-out of the historical Mary was amazingly effective. Among the Christian writers after the New Testament, the so-called Apostolic Fathers—names like Clement, Polycarp, Barnabas, Papias, Hermas—only Ignatius of Antioch (c. 100) even mentions Mary, and only rarely. One pious writer praises Ignatius in this regard for being "faithful to his convictions concerning the mystical value of silence." Notably, of Ignatius's four scant references to Mary, three emphasize that Jesus is of the "seed" and "race" of David "according to the flesh" *through* his mother, Mary—that is her singular role. It is obvious, given their ascetic tendencies toward sex and the body, that they found her a "worthy vessel" for bearing "Christ." In fact, the real Mary was busy being the consummate Jewish mother, making sure her sons and daughters were properly educated and inspired to participate in this revolution that only God could bring about.

When the curtain lifts on Mary in the early third century, with the publication of the so-called Protoevangelium of James, her transformation is complete as the virginal mother of Jesus, her other children attributed to a "previous wife" of Joseph.

Finally, as we have noted, even Joseph is denied any kind of sex life—even before his marriage to Mary. As a result, his fictitious "previous wife" disappears, and the children are then passed on to a sister-in-law of Mary's—the wife of a brother of Joseph's named Clopas. The driving idea behind this transformation is that the Holy Family must have nothing to do with sexuality.

When this grand makeover was complete, Mary was needed for only one thing: to be the pure vessel, or earthly conduit, for the incarnation of Christ, the divine Son of God. For that role, the only thing required was the "purity" of her perpetual virginity and her apolitical piety. Nothing else mattered.

Statue of Joseph, Mary, and the child Jesus
outside Sisters of Nazareth Convent

When one picks up a copy of the New Testament and begins reading the Gospels in order—Matthew, Mark, Luke, and John, followed by the book of Acts—it is important to realize two things. First, even though these works tell us about the life and career of Jesus, they are among our *latest* sources in the New Testament—all of them were written forty to seventy years after the crucifixion of Jesus in AD 30. By that time, Peter, Paul, and James are dead, and a new generation has replaced them.

These later accounts come about after the entire Jewish world that Mary lived and died in was fundamentally destroyed because of the Jewish-Roman War (66–73). John the Baptizer, Jesus, Mary, and James were all dead, as were Peter and Paul and most of the apostles. The leadership of the movement, headquartered in Jerusalem for the past forty years, had been crushed and dispersed. Emerging Christianity became centered in Antioch, Ephesus, Alexandria, and Rome—the four major urban centers of the Roman Empire. Most of its adherents were no longer Jewish. Paul's version of the Christian faith, centering on heavenly salvation through the atoning sacrifice of Jesus, largely replaced the original message of the kingdom of God being manifest on earth as a force of political and cultural transformation.

Mary is nearly absent in Mark, our earliest Gospel. The author has no problem with Jesus being the son of Mary or having brothers and sisters (Mark 6:3). In fact, without Mark we would not even know the names of all four of the brothers. But Mark marginalizes Mary and her family with two back-to-back stories—picked up by both Matthew and Luke.

Mark related that early on in Jesus's preaching career, his "kinsmen" or "family" came and took hold of him, for they said "he is beside himself"—meaning he has lost his mind (Mark 3:21). The Greek text uses a phrase that literally means "the ones with him," which does not specifically mean family, as many translations have it. That incident is immediately followed by another, in which Jesus's mother and brothers are standing outside a house so crowded with his followers that they can't even get in. Jesus is told, "Your mother and your brothers are outside, asking for you," and he replies, "Who are my mother and my brothers?" Looking around at the crowd, he declares, "Here are my mother and my brothers! Whoever does the will of God is my brother, and sister, and mother" (Mark 3:31–35). This story, along with another statement in the Gospel of John, where we read, "For even his brothers did not believe in him" (John 7:5), gave rise to the notion that Jesus's mother and family either considered him crazy or did not support his preaching and message, or both. Although the Gospel of John mentions Jesus's mother several times, he never calls her by name, and during the wedding at Cana, Jesus replies to her suggestion that the guests are out of wine with "Woman, what have you to do with me?" (John 2:1–11).

I think the weight of evidence goes the other way. I don't see any of these texts supporting the idea that Jesus's mother and family rejected him. In fact, they stand with him to the end—not only at the cross as witnesses of his suffering and death but attending to his proper burial, perhaps at risk to their own lives (Mark 15:40–16:1; John 19:25–27). Each of these texts has been misread. Mark's reference to those who thought he had lost his mind, in context clearly does not mean his immediate family, as his mother and brothers show up later at the house in Capernaum where they are staying—likely belonging to Peter. Since it is so crowded they could not even enter, Jesus in effect says *"mi casa es su casa"* to the crowd—you don't have to leave to make room for my family, *all are welcome here as my family.* As for his brothers not initially "believing" in him in John's Gospel, that is not surprising, as the author uses "believe" to mean the full faith that even the apostles were slow to come to. Jesus is head of the family, and his mother and his family travel with him and even settle in Capernaum, which becomes his headquarters in Galilee (John 2:12; Mark 3:31). Finally, the phrase Jesus uses at the wedding at Cana, translated in some versions as "Woman, what have you to do with me?" can be understood as "Should this be something that concerns us?" And addressing her as "woman" is a term of respectful address, not distance or disrespect.

That said, there is in fact a general playing down of the family's importance and a scarcity of references to Mary in the New Testament writings. I am convinced this has to do with the historical prominence of her son James—rather than Peter or Paul. This very phenomenon is in fact evidence of how important they were. In other words, it is theologically driven. It is part of a trend in all the post–AD 70 New Testament Gospels to play down the role of Jesus's human family and the Jewish side of things, largely superseded by Paul's new gospel to all humankind. And once the idea took hold of Mary as "ever virgin," there was even more reason to mute any influence of the Jesus family—since no such family even existed. Devotion to Mary was fine, but nothing involving either sex or any rival to Peter and Paul as the two central apostles of early Christianity. And along with Mary's prominence, the role of her son James as well as the leadership role of the band of women she led, including Mary Magdalene, was muted and in most cases entirely eliminated, even as early as the book of Acts. What is notable is not that they play a minimal or even nonsupportive role but that the Gospel writers know that they must still have them present—whether at the headquarters of the movement in Capernaum in Galilee, or later in Jerusalem.

Once we move into the later second century, we begin to see an obsession with Mary's bodily purity and her perpetual virginity. Her veneration is akin to that given to the various saints in the early church, who took vows of celibacy and lived an ascetic life with an emphasis on denying all bodily

The coronation of the Virgin

pleasures and instincts. Stephen Shoemaker's pioneering work, *Mary in Early Christian Life and Devotion*, has provided us with a reliable historical roadmap to these unfolding developments. Shoemaker shares my view that the de-emphasis of Mary in the New Testament is a product of an aversion to the family of Jesus, the towering influence of James, and an advocacy for Pauline Christianity.

Mary's unique role in the New Testament Gospels of Matthew and Luke centers on the virginal conception of Jesus, implying a pregnancy without sexual intercourse. As Mary says to the angel Gabriel, "How shall this be, since I know no man" (Luke 1:34). Matthew explicitly says that Joseph "knew her not" until her first son was born. Mary is revered and honored as the one chosen to bear the "Son of God," and Gabriel addresses her accordingly: "Hail, O favored one, the Lord is with you" (Luke 1:28). This is the extent of her "veneration," if one could call it that—as a favored chosen "vessel." She is the human instrument through which Jesus the divine Son of God is incarnated as a human being. Based upon these texts, early Christians of the second century AD, including Justin Martyr, Ignatius, and Irenaeus, affirmed what has come to be called the "virgin birth." Mary was the new Eve, one who reversed the curse of sin brought on by Eve's primordial disobedience.

The apocryphal Protoevangelium of James, that I briefly mentioned earlier, laid the foundation for an entirely new phase of "Marian" devotion that is with us to this day. Its major themes represent an entirely *new* view of Mary, with none of its key concepts based upon anything in the New Testament. Here is an overview of these extraordinary new perceptions of her:

- Mary's mother, Anna, becomes pregnant with Mary while her father, Joachim, is away praying and fasting for forty days in the desert for just such a child. They had sought this to the point of despair. An angel of the Lord tells Anna, "You will conceive and give birth and your child will be spoken of everywhere." When Joachim returns home, she informs him that she is with child! (Chapters 1–4)
- Mary walks at just six months old and is never allowed to touch the ground—she is raised in a bedroom away from all earthly contamination. At age three, she is taken to the temple in Jerusalem and delivered to the priests so she can be raised in perfect

holiness. She is fed like a dove, receiving food from
the hand of an angel. (Chapters 7–8)

- When Mary is twelve, ready to become a woman, the
priests of the temple fear she will defile the temple
if she begins to menstruate, so a search is made
throughout the kingdom of Judea to find the right
husband for her. Joseph is supernaturally chosen—
he is elderly, with sons and daughters from his
deceased wife. Joseph marries her and protects her as
a temple virgin, acting as her guardian and provider.
(Chapter 9)

- Mary is visited by an angel and told she will become
pregnant and give birth to the "Son of the Most
High," whom she will name Jesus. Once Joseph
discovers her pregnancy, he is in despair, thinking
he has failed his charge to ensure her purity. She
assures him that she has never known a man. Mary
is questioned by the high priests but insists on her
purity, despite their suspicions that Joseph has defiled
her. She is sent away into the desert to die, but comes
back unharmed, is declared innocent, and returns to
Joseph's house. (Chapters 11–16)

- Mary gives birth to Jesus in a cave in Bethlehem
surrounded by light. The midwife declares that
she is still a virgin—even after the birth. A woman
named Salome—presumably one of Joseph's older
children—inserts her finger into Mary's body to
verify if she is "intact" and her hand is burnt with
fire, but she is then healed. (Chapter 19–20)

The text closes with a first-person testimony by James, who
claims to be the author, as an adult child of Joseph: "I, James,

wrote this history when there was unrest in Jerusalem, at the time Herod died."

Though the Protoevangelium is very much a legendary, apocryphal text, full of wonders and fantasia, it reflects some of the key dogmas that emerge as the cornerstone of Mariology as subsequently defined by the Roman and Greek Catholic Church—namely, Mary's immaculate conception, the virgin birth of Jesus, and Mary's perpetual virginity. Whether the "brothers and sisters" of Jesus are older children of Joseph, as affirmed in the East, or children of Joseph's brother, as maintained in the West, the bottom line is clear. Mary, the mother of Jesus, never had sexual intercourse throughout her life, and her only son—Jesus—was conceived by the Holy Spirit, not because of sexual relations with a man. The church fathers are obsessed with this idea, which they understood to be the essential core of Mary's purity in body and soul and her spiritual worthiness. Joseph is consistently said to be an old man, far past an age when he would take another wife. Epiphanius asks, "How could Joseph dare to have relations with the Virgin Mary who was of such and so great holiness?" To him, the very thought is thoroughly disgusting. There are dozens of other such texts, from Origen to Tertullian to Jerome, all of which find the idea of Mary as a fully sexual woman incompatible with any sort of true spirituality—and thus unimaginable.

This vein of thinking about human sexuality reflects two separate currents that ran deep in the ancient world. The first, and more obvious, is the cultural outlook of the patriarchy. These church theologians, who are invariably male, share the common negative perceptions of women as intellectually inferior, emotionally unstable, and prone to sexual weakness as either tempted or temptress. As the apostle Paul—or one of his followers—put things:

Let a woman learn in silence with all submissiveness.
I permit no woman to teach or to have authority over
men; she is to keep silent. For Adam was formed first,
then Eve; and Adam was not deceived but the woman
was deceived and became a transgressor. Yet woman will
be saved through bearing children, if she continues in
faith and love and holiness with modesty. (I Timothy
2:11–15)

Mary's appointment as the new Eve would reverse the immorality and disobedience of her foremother who led humanity astray. For these church fathers, this meant one thing—an ascetic celibacy. Marriage was allowed, but it was certainly not the ideal state for a woman who aspired to holiness and purity of both body and spirit (I Corinthians 7:34).

The second current might be broadly called Hellenistic dualism. Dualism, simply put, is the idea that each of us— our essential "self"—is an immaterial, immortal spirit or soul, "fallen" into this material world, trapped in a material body. Human life is, accordingly, fundamentally displaced. While we are "in the body," we can never experience true light or life, which is beyond the planetary spheres ruled by tutelary demonic forces. Some of the oldest prayers for the dead in Hades are engraved on thin strips of gold and placed in the grave by the ear of the deceased. They remind the soul as it approaches the guardians of the lower Hadean world to declare boldly: "I am a child of earth and starry heaven, but *heaven alone is my home.*" Those who so "know themselves" are permitted to free themselves from Hades and the material world below and find their true home in heaven with the gods. This is the core idea of "gnostic" thinking—*knowing* this fundamental truth about the human place in the cosmos.

This basic kind of dualism takes many forms but finds its

classic expression in Plato's *Phaedo* and his cosmic work called the *Timaeus*. Many of these church fathers were deeply affected by Neoplatonism, a revived form of Plato's ancient philosophy. Next to Christ and the apostles, Plato was a close second as a spiritual model. An ascetic denial of the body—especially sexual pleasures and procreation—is the pathway to the purity to which the soul aspires. Augustine—who had a child with his unnamed lover—battled with his own sexual temptations for years while aspiring to live an ascetic, nonsexual life. His *Confessions* remains the classic reflection of his personal struggles to achieve the holiness he equated with celibacy. He was stridently insistent that Mary was a virgin throughout her life and held her up as the ideal.

These later interpretations that focused on celibacy were driven by theological dogma and constructed within a patriarchal hierarchy that viewed celibacy as the mark of a life truly devoted to God in holiness. These later Christian writers were obsessed with maintaining Mary's virginity and bodily purity, to the point of denying even her normal bodily functions like urination, defecation, and menstruation. She was likened to an angel, beyond the human even from birth. Gradually the idea developed that Mary not only became pregnant with Jesus without sexual intercourse, but remained *semper virgo*—ever a virgin—her entire life. Thus we have the utterly bizarre tale of Mary being examined for signs of virginity by a midwife *after* Jesus's birth and being declared *virgo intacta*.

At the church Councils of Ephesus (431) and Chalcedon (451), the full declaration of Mary as *Theotokos*—the God Bearer, or "Mother of God"—was adopted as official dogma, and the unshakable pillars upon which it rested were the immaculate conception, the virgin birth, and Mary's perpetual virginity. These theologians could not accept that the incarnation—God being born as a man—could come about through a woman who lived a normal human life. That she was Jewish they could not deny. But for her to have been married with children was inconceivable.

Since we don't know when Mary died, we cannot be sure if she lived long enough to experience the worst that was coming, including the brutal killing of her son James, who was thrown from the walls of Jerusalem and beaten and stoned to death by a gang of priestly opponents in AD 63. But she had surely had her fill of the bloody cruelties of the time, stretching from her childhood in Sepphoris to the rise and fall of the fanatical Herod the Great. One of our earliest sources, the church father Epiphanius, late in the fourth century, writes that he can find no tradition related to Mary's death, even though he says that he has searched the records of his day. The traditional date of Mary's death, followed by her bodily assumption to heaven, is celebrated today as August 15, AD 48. However, we have no historical sources for this date or year.

It is entirely possible that she lived into the 60s AD, when she would have been in her eighties. The Gospel of Luke tells us of an older widow named Anna, who was eighty-four (Luke 2:36). Had she died much earlier than AD 70, it is more likely there would be a record preserved, but once the Jewish revolt against the Romans broke out in AD 66, it is much less likely any record of her death would have survived. It is often assumed that people in the time of Jesus were old at fifty, but we know of many individuals in the ancient Greco-Roman world who lived into their seventies and eighties—not only the elites, but commoners as well. The mortality rates often asserted are calculations of average ages. Given the high infant and child mortality rate in the ancient world, that "average" means little. We know from both texts and archaeological evidence that if a child made it through adolescence into adulthood, living into the sixties, seventies, and eighties was not uncommon.

Ironically, it was Mary's death, and not her life, that began to generate the theological dogma that transformed her from a woman and mother into the Virgin Queen of Heaven. What was to happen to her body? How could her earthly remains decompose like any other mortal's when she was the mother of the divine Son of God, whose body, it was believed, never suffered decay? The idea of Mary's body decomposing and crumbling into dust was as distasteful to later Christianity as were her sexuality and her natural bodily functions. As a result, what happened to Mary's body after she died has been shrouded in a thick mist of theological affirmations and devotional piety.

The traditional Tomb of the Virgin in Jerusalem, near the Garden of Gethsemane at the foot of the Mount of Olives, was first venerated as a Church of Mary in the fifth century and was variously thought to be her house, her tomb, or both. Pilgrims visit parts of the structure today, but what they can see goes back only to the Crusader period. Little remains from earlier centuries.

Up the slopes of Mount Zion, a few hundred yards from our dig site, is the massive Dormition Abbey, now the highest structure on Mount Zion, just across from the Upper Room, or Cenacle. "Dormition" is taken from the Latin *dormire,* "to sleep." The abbey is Benedictine and marks the traditional spot where Mary died. Built in 1910 on land acquired by Kaiser Wilhelm in 1898, the abbey now covers the site of the fifth-century Byzantine Basilica of Hagia Sion and the twelfth-century Crusader Abbey of Our Lady, both dedicated to Mary. The central area of the abbey is a circular church with two spiral staircases leading down fifteen feet below present ground level to a crypt with a carved wooden image of Mary's body laid out in the spot where she is said to have died. Stephen Shoemaker has exhaustively researched what we know of the death of Mary, and our best evidence places her in that very location.

The death of the Virgin

Both Roman Catholic and Eastern Orthodox Christianity assert that although Mary "fell asleep" on Mount Zion, she was taken *bodily* to heaven after three days (the assumption), leaving her tomb empty—much like her son Jesus's. This teaching that Mary's physical body could not experience corruption was connected to the idea of her "immaculate" conception, referring to the doctrine that she was born without "original sin" inherited from Adam, and that her very body provided a sacred womb for Jesus as the Son of God to enter history. It was a major step in her near complete transformation from a Jewish woman of her day to a divine heavenly being, second only to Jesus Christ.

While this doctrine of the bodily assumption of the Virgin Mary was not officially defined as an infallible dogma until 1950, by Pope Pius XII, the Catholic Church both West and East affirms it. Catholics have celebrated her assumption since the fifth century on August 15 each year. What the dogma affirms is that the Virgin Mary, "having completed the course of her earthly life, was assumed body and soul into heavenly glory." Given Mary's holiness, and her unique role in bringing salvation to the world, the notion that her body would be left behind was unthinkable.

On March 27, 1980, a new historical possibility emerged, thanks to a bulldozer. A family tomb dating to the time of Jesus was exposed by the dynamite blasts of a condominium-building project just south of Mount Zion, across the Hinnom Valley in the Jerusalem neighborhood called East Talpiot. This cave tomb, quite typical of tombs in the Jerusalem of that period, was one of three on an ancient estate on the ridge. From its height you can see Jerusalem to the north and Bethlehem to the south. It was carved into the bedrock with the bones of the family members placed in ossuaries. Six of the ten ossuaries had names inscribed that uncannily echo those of Jesus and his family, including a Jesus son of Joseph, a Yose, a Maria, and a Mariamne.

The archaeologists who were called to the site in 1980 paid no particular attention to this tomb, carrying out a hastily organized weekend "rescue excavation" so that the condo building could proceed. When asked about the names much later, in 1996, when the BBC got wind of the tomb and wanted to do an Easter story on it, the main excavator responded that they were extremely common, and that of the several thousand or so tombs from that period around Jerusalem, many had these same names. Although several of the names are indeed common, their grouping in one tomb is what makes it unique. In fact, of the over six hundred inscribed ossuaries from the period, of which we have record, no other tomb has anything close to this combination of names, or could even arguably be that of the Jesus family.

The ten ossuaries inside were removed and added to the collection of the State of Israel, and the bones were turned over to the Orthodox Jewish organization responsible for Jewish burials and interred in a common field with other "unknowns."

But then the picture drastically changed. In 2002, an additional ossuary, inscribed "James, son of Joseph, brother of Jesus," surfaced in the hands of a private collector who bought it from an antiquities dealer in the Old City. Recent geochemical soil tests support the idea that this James ossuary was removed from this very tomb—when or by whom we are not sure. The results of these discoveries, including ongoing DNA and other scientific tests, potentially shed light on a whole new understanding of Mary, her family, and her death and burial in Jerusalem.

I first entered this 1980 tomb, now empty, in 2005, using only a flashlight to cut through the darkness underground. The tomb is nine by nine feet—the size of a small bedroom—and is cut into the bedrock ten feet below modern ground level. I had to squeeze through the tiny square entrance and crouch inside because the ceiling is just four feet high. In structure and feel, the tomb remained much as it had in Mary's time. I remember sitting in silence for the longest time, trying to take in where I was. I could not help wondering if I had come full circle. I had begun my quest for the historical Mary in libraries, studying ancient texts decades ago. Had I finally ended my search in the place where her surviving sons and daughters had laid her body to rest? I ran some of the loose soil through my fingers, soil that had been undisturbed since ancient times. It gave off a pungent earthy odor.

Those moments in the tomb inspired me with a renewed devotion to resurrect a more accurate historical memory of this remarkable woman. Whether this tomb, or another yet to be discovered, might be tied to Jesus's family, the experience powerfully connected to my quest for the lost Mary. Being in Jerusalem, perhaps at the place where her body was buried, was like clasping hands with Mary and her family across the millennia. But beyond her death, we now return to her life.

My depiction of this patriarchal erasure and betrayal of the historical Mary comes not from any desire to attack the teachings of the church or to offend those millions who view Mary through such theological lenses. My primary concern is that the brave Jewish girl atop the Notre Dame Center in Jerusalem, holding her baby aloft as she gazes over that troubled city, can yet find her authentic voice again—and be heard, not just by Christians, Jews, and Muslims but throughout the entire world, taking her rightful place as one of the most influential women in human history.

Chapter Ten

MARY'S MESSAGE, THEN AND NOW

He has put down the mighty from their thrones and exalted those of low degree; he has filled the hungry with good things, and the rich he has sent away empty.

—Mary

I have titled this chapter "Mary's Message," because I am convinced that a strong case can be made that Jesus's mother Mary is not only at the heart and soul of what scholars call "the Jesus Movement" but also the glue that held it together. I think there is a direct correlation between Mary the matriarch, as I have referred to her throughout the book, and the unified core message that our Gospels attribute to John the Baptizer, Jesus, and James. Our earliest text in this regard is found in the first public words that come out of Jesus's mouth in Mark, our earliest Gospel: "The time is fulfilled, and the kingdom of God is at hand, repent, and believe in the gospel" (Mark 1:15). Mark identifies this "announcement" in the previous verse as "the gospel of God" (Mark 1:14).

The Greek word translated "gospel"—*euvangelion*—is not a religious or theological term. It is used regularly for official proclamations of rulers at that time. The emperor Augustus, for example, is described as bringing the "gospel" or good news of the Pax Romana—the Roman Peace—to the world. We have an inscription from AD 9 found in Asia Minor which declares that the Gods have set things in most perfect order in sending Augustus as a "savior" to benefit humankind, and that his birth is the "beginning of the good news (*euvangelion*)" of the end of wars and "arranging all things."

Scholars pursuing the historical Jesus during the past one hundred and fifty years have failed to consider the possibility that what we identify as the revolutionary "Gospel" of Jesus goes back to Mary. Their efforts were born in the nineteenth century, when women were largely marginalized from the academy, the church, and society at large. Women filled the role of helping and assisting the men in accomplishing great things. They might be credited with supportive influence, but always in the background, never as primary leaders.

I think these scholars had things backwards. The quest for the historical Mary lies at the heart of any attempt to recover the messages of John the Baptizer, Jesus, and James, and thereby recover the nature and essence of earliest Christianity. The teaching and activities of Jesus released a mighty spiritual force that continues to have transformative power in our own time, but I am convinced that the wellspring of that force is most likely Mary herself. I would go so far as to say that Mary embodies that mighty spiritual force. Her life, her harrowing experiences, her trials, and her resolute courage as a single mother of eight in a time of great hope and great despair, served as the movement's central inspiration. As the mother of its two primary leaders, and the godmother of John the Baptizer, Mary shaped and guided the Jesus movement as was customary in a family dynastic tradition and in the Jewish culture in which she was raised and brought up her children. Her store of wisdom and experience through these troubled times was paramount.

In this chapter I examine in detail what lies at the core of this "gospel" message from our earliest sources, breaking it down into major themes and emphases. But before I turn to the message itself, I want to address the question: Upon what grounds might one conclude that Jesus's mother Mary was central to the entire movement?

Understanding the early Jesus movement historically rests upon coming to terms with three primary figures—John the Baptizer, Jesus, and James—but Mary is the link to all three. It is true that Peter and Paul become the main apostles upon whom later Christianity laid its foundation. This is vividly represented today at the Vatican. At the entrance of St. Peter's Basilica, you'll find prominent statues of Saints Peter and Paul, the two apostles considered foundational to the early Church and central figures in Christianity. These statues flank the steps leading up to the basilica and are visible to visitors entering St. Peter's Square. All over Rome it is the same, with numerous statues of Peter and Paul in public spaces. Inside St. George's Church in Istanbul (formerly Constantinople), the seat of Eastern Orthodoxy, it is much the same with icons of Peter, Paul, and the apostles inside near the main altar. Mary is of course represented, but only as the ever-Virgin mother of God. James is nowhere to be seen, even though he was the undisputed leader of the movement in the decades following the execution of Jesus, with Mary at his side

John the Baptizer inaugurates the movement, Jesus picks things up from John, and, after his crucifixion, his brother James succeeds him as the undisputed messianic leader of the movement. In one of our earliest strata in the Gospels, Jesus offers the most extravagant evaluation of John the Baptizer, whom he considers his teacher. He considers him not merely a prophet but, as he puts it, "more than a prophet." He identifies him as the final prophetic "messenger" who prepares the "way" for the arrival of the kingdom of God (Luke 7:26–27). He even goes so far as to declare that "among those born of women *there is none greater than John*" (Luke 7:28). Since Jesus was "born of a woman," the implications of such a statement are clear. This declaration is so startling that it was subsequently qualified by the phrase "but he who is least in the kingdom is greater than he." Jesus received the Holy Spirit when he was baptized *by John*, whereas John was filled with the Spirit from his mother's womb (Mark 1:9–11; Luke 1:15). Subsequent Gospel accounts play down the clear implications of this relationship—for example, Matthew has John object to baptizing Jesus, suggesting that maybe Jesus should baptize him!

John is clearly Jesus's teacher and Jesus honors him as such. Apparently, Jesus's core group of disciples were originally followers of John (John 1:40–44). Mary and Jesus's brothers are explicitly mentioned as traveling with him at this time, and the clear implication is that the entire family was baptized as well, not just Jesus (John 2:12). Once Jesus joined the movement, he began a joint-baptizing campaign in Judea to the south, whereas John was working more in the north, in Galilee (John 3:22). Jesus later declared, the very last few days of his life, in the temple at Jerusalem, that whether one had accepted the message of John and been baptized was a test of faithfulness to God (Mark 11:29–33). It was John, not Jesus, who first declared to the crowds the message of repentance and the forgiveness of sins and set forth a new ethical way that was to characterize the good news of the soon-arriving kingdom: "He who has two coats, let him share with him who has none; and he who has food, let him do likewise" (Luke 3:10–11). John also addressed non-Jews, even Roman soldiers, with his message, just as Jesus later did. The famous prayer that Jesus taught his disciples—subsequently known as the "Lord's Prayer"—was one that he learned from John (Luke 11:1). The two are so similar in message and mission that Herod Antipas, after he had John beheaded, wondered if Jesus might be John resurrected from the dead! (Mark 6:16). It was only *after* John's arrest by Herod Antipas that Jesus picked up the baton and began preaching John's gospel message as the new leader of the movement (Mark 1:14–15).

In the later, theologically motivated, strata embedded within our Gospels this is all reversed. Jesus is presented as the one and only Messiah, the central figure of redemption as God's only begotten divine Son. John is said to be a mere "forerunner" of Jesus, who introduces him and steps off the scene. John says he is not worthy to be even a servant who assists Jesus in dressing, and that Jesus is the greater one who must "increase" while John would "decrease" (Mark 1:7; John 3:30). These disclaimers come only in later Gospel layers, in an attempt to marginalize John's role in contrast to that of Jesus.

Likewise, as we have seen, James, the brother of Jesus, is given no prominence at all in our Gospels. He is mentioned by name only in two passing scenes, as a son of Mary (Mark 6:3; 15:40, and 16:1). I presented evidence that James is the mysterious unnamed "disciple whom Jesus loved," to whom Jesus passed on the care of his mother, and the undisputed leadership of the movement. Jesus says he will not leave the disciples as orphans but would send another teacher, identified in the Gospel of Thomas as James the Just, brother of Jesus (compare John 14:16, 26; Gospel of Thomas 12). Jesus and James grow up together, being nourished from the "same milk," as the Second Apocalypse of James puts it (50:18–22). And that "milk" is clearly the spiritual teachings of Mary their mother. Even in the book of Acts, which downplays the family of Jesus,

James is clearly in charge of the entire movement and supports openly the inclusion of Gentiles, accepting their repentance and faith without requiring them to become Jews—as did John the Baptizer and Jesus (Acts 15:19–21). Our one glimpse into the teachings of James, the brother of Jesus, is his letter in the New Testament, tucked away near the end and seldom read or studied. It is every bit as powerful as the Sermon on the Mount (Matthew 5–8; Luke 6:12–49). Its phrases, like the little bit we have from John the Baptizer, have a very familiar ethical ring: Be doers of the word, not hearers only. Woe to you rich, you have laid up treasures, but your gold and silver will soon perish. Has not God chosen those who are poor in the world to be rich in faith and heirs of the kingdom which he has promised to those who love him? Draw near to God and He will draw near to you. Be pure, peaceable, gentle, open to reason, full of mercy and good fruits. A harvest of righteousness is sown in peace by those who make peace. Do not swear with any oath but let your yes be yes and your no be no. Ironically, Martin Luther declared the letter of James to be an "epistle of straw," devoid of any "gospel," which Luther equated with the message of Paul. He moved it toward the back of his German translation of the New Testament to underline its relative unimportance.

John the Baptizer's mother, Elizabeth, is part of Mary's extended family. Mary fled the village of Nazareth when she became pregnant to find solace with Elizabeth, who is described as "in her old age" but is six months pregnant with John. Mary stays with her for three months, attending at John's birth (Luke 1:39–56). It seems likely that Elizabeth and John's father, Zechariah, would have died before John reached adulthood, and as an only child John would have looked to Mary for guidance. It is even possible that Mary took him into her home. Regardless, we find him in Galilee, not in Judea, where he was born, when he first shows up as an adult in our accounts, and his first core followers—Peter, Andrew, Philip, and others are fishermen around the sea of Galilee (John 3:22–24). When Jesus gathers his disciples after John's arrest, they are not new followers but key leaders who had already been working with John as his disciples.

The bottom line is that what scholars refer to as the "Jesus movement" is a "family affair" from the start. Mary as the matriarch headed a "band of sisters," among them Mary Magdalene and many other influential women who had followed Jesus in Galilee, along with the twelve. In all our portrayals of Jesus, from movies to novels to art and church publications, we see Jesus alone with his twelve male followers, traveling about together, as if they lived on air. In fact, this large entourage of women traveled with him as well and, what's more, provided the financial support underpinning the entire group. We might properly speak of a "Jesus entourage" spearheaded by Mary. They are women of influence and means and are the backbone of the movement—including Mary Magdalene, who, like Jesus's mother, was marginalized in later tradition (Luke 8:1–3). The Gospel of Philip, discovered in 1945 in Egypt, says there were three Marys who always "walked with the Lord": his mother, his sister, and Mary Magdalene, his companion. These women stood by Jesus near the cross, as did James, even when the male disciples had fled for their lives in terror at Jesus's arrest or denied even knowing him, in the case of Peter (Luke 23:49). These women were the rock and the foundation of the movement, and without them it would not have sustained itself.

Mary was no casual observer. She was a full-stakes player in a dangerous, messianic game of thrones. We have seen how Mary's life spans the heyday of ancient Jewish messianism, from the rise of the indigenous Hasmonean royalty and Herod's attempt to become the rightful king of the Jews, through the destruction of dozens of messianic claimants and movements, to the beginnings of two great Jewish revolts against Rome that ended in utter disaster for the Jewish people and their ancestral homeland (AD 66–136). Josephus is generally negative about such attempts to overthrow Roman rule and bring about the expected "time of the end" as predicted by the Hebrew prophets. He labels these figures "brigands" or "impostors," and he explicitly says that several of them put on the "diadem"—an indication of their claim to royal messianic status, most likely as a rightful king of the line of David. That is why the term "messianic" is appropriate here. These figures surely wanted to spark a revolutionary overthrow of the Jewish ruling classes and their Roman overlords, but their intent was not merely to control the reins of political and military power but to usher in the kingdom of God, inaugurated by the manifestation of the Davidic and priestly messiahs as foretold by the prophets of the Hebrew Bible. The expectations and definitions of such an ideal kingdom likely varied, running the gamut from the political restoration of the nation of Israel independent of all foreign rule to a perfected world of peace and justice under the rule of the one God whom they believed was the creator of humankind.

Mary witnessed firsthand the mass crucifixions, beheadings, exiles, and enslavement of countless thousands of Jews. All too often, Mary's personal faith and piety have been viewed out of the context of the very real political, religious, and social world in which she and her family lived. Mary stood for a dynamic, radical, transforming political and social program that has been lost. As Hugh Schonfield put it, "The Messianism which grew into the Christian religion was rocked in a political cradle." Mary was the mind and heart of this movement. She had witnessed firsthand the disastrous truth of a principle she taught her sons; namely, that "those who live by the sword, will die by the sword." Mary's brilliant and insightful mind comes through unfiltered in the revolutionary teachings of her sons Jesus and James—and her nephew John the Baptizer. These ideas and principles did not spring from dry ground but from a well-watered garden that Mary provided for her family, even as a widowed single mother with eight or more children.

The brutal murder of three of her sons—Jesus, James, and Simon—by Roman and Jewish rulers as threats to their power and aspirations puts her at the center stage of one of the most pivotal and influential times in history. Mary's erasure, and that of her family, paved the way for the kind of revisionism that ensured a woman would not be credited with a central and pivotal role of "first founder" of the most influential movement in human history. Far too long have women with brilliant ideas and insights been diminished as thinkers, their primary role relegated to giving birth to important men. Mary was recast as the "divine vessel" for the "virgin birth" of Jesus as the divine "Son of God," and then hustled off the historical stage. Unfortunately, it is not a stretch to see a process at work here that is all too familiar to many creative women who have played decisive roles but now are relegated to the background or forgotten altogether.

This idea that Jesus's mother and family did not support his work has been enormously influential. I had an academic colleague say to me once, hearing about my project: "Isn't it obvious in the Gospels that Jesus's mother and family were alienated from him, despite the theological need to exalt Mary as his Virgin Mother in the birth stories in Matthew and Luke? Once Jesus is born, Mary plays virtually no part in any of our Gospel accounts, so how could one possibly write a book about her?" Two recent award-winning novels, Colm Tóibín's *The Testament of Mary* and Naomi Alderman's *The Liar's Gospel*, build their narratives around the idea of Mary viewing Jesus and his followers as a bunch of misfits and lunatics. While one can value such books for their literary features, I question this core assumption.

I turn now to the major themes, ideas, and emphases of this "gospel" message. Despite the later theological overlay, even in our New Testament Gospels, and the towering influence of the apostle Paul—who never even mentions Mary by name, only that Jesus was "born of a woman"—I believe the core message can be highlighted and recovered.

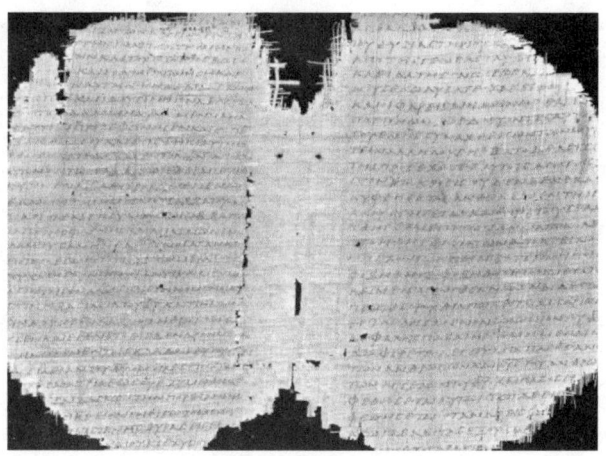

Early papyrus with teachings of
Jesus from Q Source

Scholars have developed a set of "criteria of authenticity" as a method of sorting through the multiple sayings and stories attributed to Jesus in our early sources. The idea is not to isolate all that Jesus might have said or taught, but to identify an irreducible minimum of his most characteristic teachings, thus allowing us to recover what lay at the core of the movement's revolutionary vision of the future. That in turn takes us back to Mary, as pioneer and first founder of what characteristically emerged.

One of the great "textual" discoveries that scholars have made in the past hundred years is the identification of a "hidden" collection of the sayings of Jesus that they believe was assembled before any of the New Testament Gospels were written, perhaps as early as the 50s AD. This source is commonly called Q—from the German word *Quelle*, meaning "source." We can isolate or "recover" this hypothetical text by pulling out the materials that Matthew and Luke have in common that are not in Mark. When this material is examined, it turns out to be approximately sixty units of sayings and teachings, but virtually no narrative stories. Many scholars are convinced that Jesus's earliest followers would have collected his teachings and sayings as with any rabbi of his day, probably in a single scroll. This core collection would predate the writing of any of the Gospels.

As a result of many decades of such academic work, there are areas of clear consensus among scholars. I have organized some of the major results that pass the "authenticity" test under the following five headings. Most of these texts come either from Mark, which is our earliest Gospel, or from the Q Source. The following is an overview of these major declarative themes with an extracted sample of these teachings that belong under each, along with a brief explanatory analysis.

The Kingdom of God Is Already Present but Not Yet Realized

The time is fulfilled, the kingdom of God is at hand. If I by the finger of God cast out demons, then the kingdom of God has come upon you. The kingdom of God is not coming with signs to be observed; nor will they say, "Lo here it is!" or "There!" for behold the kingdom of God is in the midst of you. You are not far from the kingdom of God. Father, let your kingdom come; let your will be done. The kingdom of God is like leaven which a woman took and hid in three measures of flour, till it was all leavened. The kingdom of God is like scattered seed, first the blade, then the ear, then the full grain in the ear; or like a grain of mustard seed, the smallest of seeds that grows up and puts forth large branches for birds to nest. The Torah and the prophets were until John but since that time the good news of the kingdom of God is preached, and everyone enters forcefully.

Simply put, the kingdom of God entailed the will of God being done on earth as it is in heaven. This was taken almost universally in the time of Mary as something that would come about only through the dramatic and forceful intervention of God in human affairs and the establishment of the rule of the priestly and royal messiahs. In the time of Mary and Jesus, it was commonly believed that the arrival of the kingdom involved the "binding of Satan," who was seen behind the evil forces operating in human affairs.

What Jesus teaches here is unique. It involves a different understanding of *eschatology*—the ideas about the final decisive events of human history, already present though ironically not yet here. Some scholars have characterized Jesus's approach to the kingdom as "realized eschatology." The kingdom of God was decisively inaugurated with the mission and message of Jesus. It was not only "at hand" but had "come upon you" and was "in your midst." Its consummation only unfolds to the degree it takes hold in individual lives and within society, fundamentally overturning the "powers that be" in a revolution that transforms the world.

2. What Is Up Is Down, and What Is Down Is Up

*Blessed are the poor, for yours is the kingdom of God; blessed are you
that hunger now, for you shall be satisfied; blessed are you that weep
now, for you shall laugh; blessed are the meek, for they shall inherit
the earth; blessed are the pure in heart, the merciful, the peacemakers,
and those persecuted, for theirs is the kingdom of God. Everyone who
has left house or brothers or sisters or mother or father or children
or lands for my sake and for the gospel of the kingdom will receive a
hundredfold now in this time—and in the age to come eternal life.
But many that are first will be last, and the last will be first. Do
not be anxious for food or clothing, for all these things the nations
of the world seek, instead seek his kingdom and all these things shall
be yours as well. Behold, those who are gorgeously appareled and
live in luxury are in king's courts. Sell your possessions and give
to all who are in need. Give to him who begs from you, and do not
refuse him who would borrow from you. He who has two coats, let
him share with him who has none; and he who has food, let him do
likewise. The kings of the Gentiles exercise lordship over them; and
those in authority over them are called benefactors. But not so with
you; rather let the greatest among you become as the youngest, and the
leaders as one who serves. Whoever would be great among you must
be your servant, and whoever would be first among you must be
slave of all. As you wish that men would do to you, do so to them,
this is the Torah and the prophets.*

In these texts we see the revolutionary idea that wealth and
political power in the service of oppression and injustice are
undercut by those who take up the challenge to live according
to a transformed set of values. The promise is that God will
empower those who so live to inaugurate an overturning of the
forces of evil in the world. As with the first theme, this is not

a transformation that takes place in a moment of time, but a permeating influence that begins to cut away at the foundations of establishment power and privilege.

3. The Internal, Not the External, Is What Counts

Religious authorities who love money justify themselves before men, but God knows their hearts; for what is exalted among men is an abomination in the sight of God. Pray or fast in secret, not publicly to be seen by people as religious. Don't make long prayers, and heap up empty phrases, for God knows your heart and your needs. When you give, don't let your left hand know what your right hand is doing. Let your gift sweat in your hands until you know to whom you give it. I came not to call the so-called righteous but sinners to repentance. Outwardly you appear righteous to me, but within you are full of corruption, decay, hypocrisy, and iniquity. The good man out of the good treasure of his heart produces good, and the evil man out of his evil treasure produces evil; for out of the abundance of the heart his mouth speaks. Do not swear with oaths, but let your yes be yes and your no be no.

This fundamental theme becomes powerfully operative as it is applied in every area of life, not only those practices that usually fall under the category of "religion," but extending into external moral judgments about the value, standing, or motivations of others, whether the socially disenfranchised tax collectors, the nonreligious who were considered "sinners," or even prostitutes. It would by extension merge with the second theme and reach into areas of politics and class, where ostentatious displays of power are prized above inner truth. I have included here the short pithy sayings of Jesus, but he also told stories and taught parables that emphasized God's unconditional forgiveness toward those whose hearts were pure. For example, the story of the tax collector and the religious Pharisee who prayed in the temple side by side (Luke 18:9–14).

4. A Transformed Egalitarian Society: Gender, Class, and Ethnicity

Truly I say to you tax collectors and harlots go into the kingdom of God before you. Go out into the streets and lanes of the city, and to the highways, and bring in the poor and maimed and blind and lame and those who are homeless for the messianic banquet. Was no one found to return and give praise to God except this foreigner— a Samaritan? This poor widow who gave two copper coins has put in more than all those who contributed out of their abundance. Truly I say to you, not even in Israel have I found such faith [spoken to a Roman centurion]. Do not swear, Mary has chosen the better part, and it shall not be taken away from her [spoken to the men sitting at the feet of Jesus as rabbi].

This theme pulls in multiple sayings, stories, and reports of Jesus's behavior that broke through societal norms. Jesus freely socializes with tax collectors and sinners, who were considered outside the sphere of religious acceptability. Tax collectors were seen as collaborators with the Roman occupation and Herodian rule. He even chooses a tax collector—Matthew— as one of the twelve. He freely deals with Samaritans, who were culturally and racially excluded from Jewish society. In what is perhaps his best-known story, he commended a "Good Samaritan" for showing that the true meaning of "Love your neighbor as yourself" knows no social or cultural boundaries. He deals openly with a "woman of the street" who, seeking a new beginning to her life, invades a wealthy dinner party where Jesus was

The Good Samaritan

the guest to anoint his feet with perfumed oil and bathe them with her tears (Luke 7:36–50).

Jesus commends Mary of Bethany, sister of Martha and Lazarus, for sitting with the male disciples listening to his teaching. The idea is not that "poor" Martha should be left with the housework—abandoned by her sister—but rather that women have intelligence and insights and can be full participants in intellectual and spiritual discussions (Luke 10:38–42). The implications of this are shattering. He freely speaks with women—including non-Jews—shocking even his disciples, who "marveled that he was talking with a woman."

The huge crowds that followed Jesus in Galilee flocked from the entire region—Judea, Samaria, and Tyre and Sidon on the coast, as well as the Hellenistic cities of the Decapolis beyond the Jordan—an incredibly diverse mixture unsegregated by gender, class, race, religion, or culture. Since Jesus was neither gathering weapons nor threatening violence against Herod Antipas—and even encouraged the paying of the tribute tax—Herod's desire to kill him, as he had done with John the Baptizer, was clearly based on this massive gathering. Josephus says as much about John's movement—that Herod was alarmed at the large crowds he was drawing—and those same crowds turned to Jesus after John's death, and then to James. Jesus's teachings and activities were a threat to societal norms and order. Both Roman and Jewish societies were highly stratified along lines of social class, economic status, and religious practice. To have rich and poor, enslaved and free, men and women, Jews and Samaritans, Romans and Greeks, all melding into one new spiritual family was more of a threat to Herod Antipas and the Romans than any number of armed messianic bands prowling the countryside and creating local havoc.

5. Love, Forgiveness, and Nonviolence Transform the World

But I say to you that hear, love your enemies, do good to those who hate you, bless those who curse you, pray for those who abuse you. To him who strikes you on the cheek, offer the other also; and from him who takes away your coat do not withhold even your shirt. If anyone forces you to go one mile, go with him two miles. All who take the sword will perish by the sword. But love your enemies, and do good, and lend, expecting nothing in return; and your reward

*will be great, and you will be sons of the Most High; for God is
kind to the ungrateful and the selfish. Be merciful, even as your
Father is merciful. Judge not and you will not be judged; condemn
not and you will not be condemned; forgive and you will be
forgiven; give and it will be given to you; good measure, pressed
down, shaken together, running over, will be put into your lap. For
the measure you give will be the measure you get back. If your
brother or sister sins against you seven times in the day, and turns
to you seven times and says, I repent, you must forgive him—even
to seventy times seven! Render to Caesar the things that are Caesar's.*

The Peaceable Kingdom

This final theme is by far the most radical of the five, particularly the mandate to respond with love and kindness in the
face of violence and injustice. "Love your enemies" and "Turn
the other cheek" have become proverbial and are generally relegated to one's personal life, if taken seriously at all. However,
the radical revolutionary political and social contexts are evi-
dent. It was the occupying Roman forces that had rights of
forcing the indigenous population to help with logistical transport, which seems to be the context for the proverbial "going

the second mile." To "render unto Caesar" involved a poll tax that the Romans required of each male.

Judas the Galilean, who founded the sect of the Zealots, incited his countrymen to revolt in AD 6 by upbraiding them as cowards for agreeing to pay this tribute to the Romans and thereby tolerating them as masters rather than God alone (*Jewish War* 2.118). In contrast, Jesus is allowing for accommodation with the occupying forces—something none of the other messiahs of Mary's time would have remotely entertained or endorsed. This, along with Jesus's prohibition on bearing arms against these enemies—whether the Herodian or the Roman authorities—sets him in radical opposition to the common understanding of the Davidic messiah. In the Dead Sea Scrolls we read how the "Branch of David" will pursue his enemies to the Mediterranean and slay the ruler of the Kittim (the Romans). A scroll that was found in Cave I that we refer to as the War Scroll foretells how the high priest and the prince of the congregation—or Davidic messiah—will utterly destroy all the "children of darkness," whether Jewish or Gentile. As the scroll puts it, "The dominion of the Kittim shall come to an end and iniquity shall be vanquished, leaving no remnant; for the sons of darkness there shall be no escape."

The Jesus movement had a drastically different view of how the kingdom of God would finally come about: "not by might, nor by power, but by my Spirit," as the prophet Zechariah put things in the sixth century BC, speaking of the coming of the two "anointed ones who stand by the Lord of the whole earth" (Zechariah 4). Jesus and his followers apparently viewed the Roman Empire, the Herodian family of rulers, and the Jewish religious establishment as a cluster of very similar agents and entities that would impede the arrival of the kingdom. The book of Daniel speaks of the kingdom as a great "stone" that grows to fill the whole earth (Daniel 2:31–35). Also, the major text in the Hebrew Prophets about the arrival of the Messiah and his kingdom imagines a gradual process, where enemies are destroyed by the "rod of his mouth," and the "breath of his lips," until the knowledge of God finally fills the earth as the waters cover the sea (Isaiah 11:4–9).

The results of recovering the historical Mary—the real Mary—can have profound implications for our world today. First and foremost, we owe it to her—as is the case with any historical figure whose life story has been lost, distorted, or transformed in such significant ways. In the case of Mary much more is at stake, since she is the most notable and recognized woman in history, whereas her image as the ever-virgin Queen of Heaven and Mother of God is so far removed from any historical reality that we can recover from our earliest sources. This theological transformation in the centuries after her life took from her the very things most important to her: Her Jewish faith. Her eight children, whom she courageously guided into adulthood as a single mother after Joseph died. Her sexuality and womanhood. The incredible courage and inspiration she provided to her most remarkable son, Jesus, and his all-but-forgotten brother James, which birthed the movement we now know as Christianity.

As such, Mary can serve as an inspiration for all of us as human beings who want to overcome this kind of historical amnesia that has afflicted our memories of human history for millennia. If we can take the best-known, least-known woman in history as our model of collective recollection and allow her to find her life again in our thoughts of her, we can only begin to imagine the inspiring results for countless women of the past. And not only the past but the present. The millions of young women who look for models of courage and inspiration in their own lives can find in Mary a vision of feminine power and influence.

The implications for Judaism are equally far-reaching. The way is open for Mary—or Miriam, as she was known in her own time—to be reclaimed as one of the greatest heroines of Jewish history—alongside Sarah, Rebecca, Rachel, Leah, Moses's sister Miriam, Deborah, Ruth, Esther, Queen Salome, and so many more. It is time for Mary to return home—to her people and to her land—honored for her courageous resistance to violence, oppression, and injustice through the movement she birthed and inspired at one of the most pivotal, violent, and troubled times in Jewish history. Her teachings and her message, which reach us through the influence of her sons Jesus and James, went international and now, along with the Ten Commandments of Moses and the precepts of the Sermon on the Mount, provide a shining moral compass to all humankind.

And Christians can find far-reaching and transformative inspiration from the historical Mary. All religious movements have "founders," whether Abraham, Moses, Buddha, Jesus, or Mohammed. The results of my research point to Mary not merely as an inspiration and influence but as the "first founder" of the movement that became Christianity. Scholars have been on a "quest for the historical Jesus" for the past two hundred years. But to understand the historical Jesus one needs to focus on recovering Mary—and with her John the Baptizer and James. These are the significant forgotten ones—momentous bookends to the life of Jesus. They are mentioned in the New Testament—given a certain restricted recognition—but their full stories, as we have seen, have been deliberately erased over time. Once Jesus is put into that wider context his life and message take on a new and dynamic relevance to human life *in this world*, in contrast to Paul's idea of "salvation" in a heavenly world to come.

Mary, leader among the apostles
on Mount Zion

The only prophetic words we have from Mary are from the Gospel of Luke, when she is first pregnant with Jesus: "God our Savior has shown strength with his arm, he has scattered the proud in the imagination of their hearts, he has put down the mighty from their thrones and exalted those of low degree; he has filled the hungry with good things, and the rich he has sent empty away" (Luke 1:51–53). Scholars might doubt that these precise words come from the historical Mary, but they nonetheless reflect the program that John the Baptizer preached, that Jesus inaugurated as a broad and diverse movement, and that his brother James carried on for over three decades after his death. To be "not far from the kingdom of God" is to have the insight and understanding to take up the way of life that Mary and her family pioneered, which alone will bring down the mighty and exalt those of low degree, bringing justice, righteousness, and peace to the earth. She and her family inaugurated this "Good News" in one of the most tumultuous times of history. Their hopes and dreams are as relevant today as they were two thousand years ago—namely, that our world could find the paths to the peace, justice, freedom, and equality for which all those of goodwill long. Only then will we recognize the true and full meaning of the ancient prayer of Mary, "For behold, henceforth all generations will call me blessed."

Acknowledgments

I have spent a decade working on this book and must thank first and foremost my marvelous agent, Doug Abrams, and the entire team at Idea Architects, one of the most creatively innovative organizations in the publishing business—their motto might well be "Have Dream, Will Travel." Doug and I go back to the early 1990s, and he has had an influential and inspiring hand in most of my book projects since. After I had completed books on Jesus and Paul, it was Doug who first suggested, Why not Mary? It was a bold and challenging idea and one that emerged in ways I could not have anticipated at the time. It was also Doug who introduced me to my editor at Knopf, Victoria Wilson, whose keen insights and enthusiasm for this project, from start to finish, have steadied my course along the way. Vicky's ability to succinctly evaluate where I found myself in this process, and to inspire me to dig deeper in recovering the lost Mary, as a scholar and writer, were invaluable. I am grateful also to Todd Portnowitz, who so graciously and skillfully took over this project as editor when Vicky retired at the end of 2023. His insightful reading of the final draft version of this book brought fresh eyes and illuminating suggestions to the project.

I must also thank my encouraging academic colleagues who

read versions of my proposed ideas and research along the way, namely Jorunn Jacobsen Buckley, Jeffrey Bütz, John Dominic Crossan, April DeConick, Arthur Droge, Eugene Gallagher, Shimon Gibson, Naomi Janowitz, Elaine Pagels, Jane Schaberg, John Shelby Spong, and Tina Wray. I am also grateful to graphic designer Daniel Wright for his work processing the photos in the book. The two scholars from whose work I most benefited, Richard Bauckham and Stephen Shoemaker, I deeply appreciate—though my conclusions are of course my own. It is not customary to mention ancient figures in one's acknowledgments, but in the case of Mary, I could have done little of what I have done without the writings of the first-century Jewish historian Josephus. All of us who work in Christian origins know that much of what we do would be irretrievably impaired without his works.

Finally, I thank my ever-encouraging family, Lori, Eve, and Seth—and our precious dogs—ever a source of inspiration, refuge, and stimulation over the many years of researching and writing this book. Mary has very much become a living part of our household, on a level none of us could have anticipated— in art, music, and endless exchanges along the way.

Notes

CHAPTER ONE: FINDING THE LOST MARY

4 I have written books on Jesus and Paul: See Tabor, *The Jesus Dynasty.*

5 Mary's entry in Wikipedia: "Mary, mother of Jesus," Wikipedia, en.wikipedia.org.

5 The great museums of Western culture: Pelikan, *Mary Through the Centuries;* Pelikan, Flusser, and Lang, eds. *Mary: Images of the Mother of Jesus.* See the extensive sample of major works archived as "Madonna structured gallery" in Wikimedia Commons, commons.wikimedia.org.

5 Mary, or Maryam in Arabic: *Sura* 19 is named "Mary," or "Maryam" in Arabic. The primary references to Mary in the Qur'an are: 3.35–47; 4.156, 171; 19.16–36; 21.91; 23.50–51, along with over twenty references to Jesus as "son of Mary."

7 Our New Testament evidence: Including parallel accounts, Mary appears in the following scenes: Jesus's genealogy (Matthew 1:16; Luke 3:23, alluded to but not named); the birth accounts of John the Baptizer and Jesus (Matthew 1:18–2:23; Luke 1–2); Jesus at age twelve in Jerusalem (Luke 2:41–52); the wedding at Cana (John 2:1–12); at Peter's house in Capernaum (Mark 3:31; Matthew 12:46; Luke 8:19–21); Jesus's rejection at Nazareth (Mark 6:1–6; Matthew 13:53–58; cf. Luke 4:16–30); at the crucifixion of Jesus (Mark 15:40–441; Matthew 27:55–56; John 19:25–27); at Jesus's burial (Mark 15:47; Matthew 27:61; Luke 23:55–56); at the empty tomb (Mark 16:1–2; Matthew 28:1; Luke 24:1–10); and finally in Jerusalem after the death of Jesus on the day of Pentecost with Jesus's brothers and the apostles (Acts 1:14).

8 I could not count the times: Jesus's four brothers are named in Mark 6:3, our earliest Gospel, along with a reference to his "sisters," who are not named. Mark also knows a Salome, who assists Mary Magdalene and

Jesus's mother Mary with Jesus's burial (Mark 15:40; 16:1). She might well be one of the sisters, given that family members buried their dead. The other two, Miriam/Mary and Anna, we know only from later sources; see Epiphanius, *Panarian* 78:8,1; 9,6. In another work Epiphanius names Anna and Salome (*Ancoratus* 60.1). So, all told, we can account for a large family of at least eight children, five boys and three girls: Jesus, James, Joses, Jude, Simon, Salome, Mary, and Anna.

9 Several Gospel texts describe Jesus: Luke 2: 42–52 and Mark 2:1; 3:31– 32; 6:3; John 2:12; 19:26–27. On these so-called lost years of Jesus, see my lecture "The Lost Years of Jesus Revealed—at Last!," James Tabor channel, YouTube.

9 And when James was brutally stoned: The horribly violent death of James is recounted by the church historian Eusebius, who quotes an earlier Jewish Christian writer of the mid–second century, Hegesippus. James was thrown off the southeast wall of the temple enclosure into the Kidron Valley below, and then stoned and beaten to death with clubs. His brother Simon was looking on (*Church History* 2.23.3–18). Simon is said to have lived past the age of one hundred and was crucified in the ninth or tenth year of the reign of the emperor Trajan (AD 106 or 107), to eliminate members of the Davidic family (Eusebius, *Church History* 3.11.1; 3.22.3–4; 3:32.3–7). Although some texts make him a "cousin" of Jesus, to support the idea that Mary remained a "perpetual virgin," our best evidence is that he is a brother.

11 It became important to deemphasize: On this deemphasis of the family of Jesus in the interest of promoting his divinity see Stephen Shoemaker, *Mary in Early Christian Faith and Devotion*, as well as my book *The Jesus Dynasty*, Barrie Wilson's *How Jesus Became Christian*, and Bart Ehrman's *How Jesus Became God*.

11 Leading scholars and historians: See the pioneering studies of Fiorenza, *In Memory of Her*; Schaberg, *The Illegitimacy of Jesus*; and Levine, ed., *A Feminist Companion to Mariology*.

12 To her and to all: I am thinking here of Franz Schubert's incomparable "Ave Maria," composed in 1825 to a text from the German translation of Walter Scott's poem *The Lady of the Lake*, and its piano arrangement by Franz Liszt. The lyrics have varied with many renditions, including the English version of the third stanza written by Rachel Field for Walt Disney's *Fantasia* (1940), which so captures the very human Mary I have sought to recover.

CHAPTER TWO: TWO THOUSAND CRUCIFIXIONS

13 The corpses were left: In Jewish law the burial of the dead, including enemies, was of utmost importance, and leaving a corpse left unburied was a shameless act of humiliation (Deuteronomy 21:22–23, 28:25–26; Jeremiah 7:33). Roman crucifixion, in contrast, saw leaving the corpse hanging for carrion birds and beasts to devour as part of the shame of the punishment (Suetonius, *Augustus* 13:1–2). In all four of our New Testament Gospels the Roman governor of Judea, Pontius Pilate, who served under the emperor Tiberius from c. AD 26 to 36, grants an influential member of the Jewish Sanhedrin, Joseph of Arimathea, permission to bury Jesus. A few New Testament scholars, notably John Dominic Crossan, have asserted that the account of Jesus's burial by Joseph of Arimathea is likely invented, with Joseph a completely fictional character, and part of the "empty tomb" idea that developed around affirmations of Jesus's resurrection. Crossan thinks it likely that Jesus would have either been left on the cross or thrown into a shallow grave. In either case, his body would have been consumed by dogs or jackals. See Crossan, *Jesus: A Revolutionary Biography* (New York: HarperCollins, 1994), 123–158. John Granger Cook finds Crossan's evidence unconvincing; see "Crucifixion and Burial," *New Testament Studies* 57, no. 2 (2011): 193–213. Craig A. Evans devotes three chapters in his book *Jesus and the Remains of His Day* to the subject, arguing the same—namely, that the Romans allowed proper burial of victims, especially given Jewish sensibilities regarding corpse exposure. On crucifixion in the ancient Mediterranean world there are the massive studies of Gunnar Samuelsson, *Crucifixion in Antiquity*, and John Granger Cook, *Crucifixion in the Mediterranean World*.

14 It was the summer: Contrary to common perceptions, there is no year "zero" in our BC/AD system of reckoning dates before and after the birth of Jesus. Further, due to adjustments for accuracy in our modern Gregorian calendar, the birth of Jesus was neither 1 BC nor AD 1, but in the fall of 5 BC, based on our current reckoning. The Gregorian calendar, introduced by Pope Gregory XIII in 1582, was a corrected refinement of the older Julian calendar. We don't have a record of the precise age of Mary at Jesus's birth in 5 BC, but since it was common for parents to arrange marriages for their daughters around the age of fourteen, I have put her birth in 19 BC.

14 Joseph was not the father: Jesus is called "the son of Joseph" two times in the Gospel of John, and "Joseph's son" once in Luke (John 1:45, 6:42; Luke 4:22). However, in Mark, our earliest New Testament Gospel, he is referred to as the "son of Mary" (Mark 6:3). This designation, coming

from our earliest source, seems to reflect some kind of aversion to the idea that Jesus was the biological son of Joseph.

14 "And when they had performed": Translations from the Bible and Apocrypha are from *The New Oxford Annotated Bible with the Apocrypha*, Revised Standard Version, Expanded Edition (New York: Oxford University Press, 1977). Emphases are mine throughout.

15 Matthew also tells of their settling: Most historians consider the Matthew stories to be legendary, based on his attempt to fulfill two obscure references in the Hebrew prophets, neither of which has anything to do with Jesus in its historical context: "Out of Egypt I have called my son" (Hosea 11:11/Matthew 2:15) and "He shall be called a Nazarene" (possibly based on Isaiah 11:1/Matthew 2:23). Our best evidence puts Jesus's birth in the fall of 5 BC—with Herod the Great's death the following spring. The evidence is complicated, but here is a useful summary: "A Historian's Take on a Different Kind of 'Silent Night,'" Taborblog, jamestabor.com. Other years have been proposed, including 6 BC, based on astrological factors; see Molnar, *The Star of Bethlehem*. For a survey of all the main proposed dates, with arguments pro and con, see Finegan, *Handbook of Biblical Chronology*, 279–328.

15 Herod the Great: Our primary witness for this period is Josephus and his two major works, *The Jewish War* and *Jewish Antiquities*. References to Josephus are from the editions *Jewish War*, trans. by H. St. J. Thackeray, Loeb Classical Library (Cambridge, MA: Harvard University Press, 1927), and *Jewish Antiquities*, trans. by Allen Wikgren, Loeb Classical Library (Cambridge, MA: Harvard University Press, 1943). For further general study on Josephus and his times I recommend the excellent and accessible volume by Steve Mason, *Josephus and the New Testament*, 2nd ed. (Ada, MI: Baker Academic, 2022), along with Mason's half-dozen other books and numerous articles.

17 Herod had left several wills: Antipas and Archelaus were brothers, sons of Herod's wife Malthace, who was a Samaritan. She died in 4 BC, in Rome, while the two brothers were vying for power (Josephus, *Jewish War* 1.561). Philip was the son of another wife of Herod, Cleopatra—not the Egyptian ruler but sharing that name. He is mentioned in Luke 3:1 and is usually called "Philip the Tetrarch" to distinguish him from another son of Herod named Philip—usually called Philip I—son of Herod's wife Mariame, the second wife by that name. We think it is Philip I, not the Tetrarch, who was married to the beautiful Herodias, whom Herod Antipas married and who was condemned by John the Baptizer for adultery, leading to his beheading (Mark 6:17–18).

17 One month after Herod's death: Josephus, *Jewish War* 2.10–13, is our source for what follows here.

18 The Gospel of Luke tells us: What percentage of the Jewish population of the land of Israel made these pilgrim festival journeys we cannot be sure, but we know many did, as circumstances permitted, especially since the Torah commands that all Israelite males be present in Jerusalem for the three main festivals (Exodus 23:14–17; Deuteronomy 16:16–17); see Samuel Safrai, "Pilgrimage in the Time of Jesus," Jerusalem Perspective, September 1, 1989, jerusalemperspective.com. These festivals were not like the Muslim hajj—a once-in-a-lifetime requirement that one travel to Mecca—but a regular annual cycle of holy days, namely, Passover (Pesach), Pentecost (Shavuot), and the celebration of Tabernacles (Sukkoth), as commanded in the Torah (Deuteronomy 16:16–17). Josephus claims that at Passover alone, there were upwards of three million people gathered in Jerusalem (*Jewish War* 2.280). Although most scholars would see this as an exaggeration, which Josephus tends to do when dealing with crowds, battles, and casualties, the number was nonetheless vast, and no other gatherings in the country would rival these festivals.

19 The expanded temple courtyard: This estimate assumes four square feet per person and is only a guess. Crowd estimates of Muslim pilgrims on the Haram—where the parameters of Herod's temple are still visible—number over a quarter million during Ramadan.

20 Generally, after a major Jewish festival: The only story we have of Jesus as a child in the New Testament Gospels is the account in Luke where Jesus at age twelve gets left behind in Galilee as the family headed back to Nazareth after the eight-day festival of Passover and the Days of Unleavened Bread. According to the story his parents did not miss him, assuming he was with the village entourage that had traveled together (Luke 2:41–51).

20 Fifty days later: Josephus, *Jewish War* 2.42–44.

22 Judas's father . . . Hezekiah: Josephus, *Jewish War* 2.56. Josephus reports that in AD 6, when Herod's son Archelaus, ruler of Judea, was banished by the emperor Augustus, one "Judas the Galilean" raised a similar rebellion (*Jewish War* 2.117–118; *Jewish Antiquities* 18.4; Acts 5:37). Some scholars have identified him with Judas the son of Hezekiah, but this seems unlikely, since Josephus, our primary source for the period, places that Judas earlier, in 4 BC, after the death of Herod the Great.

22 The Romans had a well-practiced way: The Jewish ruler Antigonus, for example, was apparently crucified and then beheaded by Marc Antony after he was captured by Herod the Great when Herod was consolidating his power in 37 BC.

23 As such he had been assigned to: Varus was responsible for the devastating Roman defeat in the Teutoburger Forest, east of the Rhine, in AD 9 by the German Arminius, who had him killed, changing the course of history. The Romans lost three legions in what became known as the "Varus

Disaster" (*Clades Variana*). Varus was married to the grandniece of the emperor Augustus and was well connected in aristocratic Roman circles. According to the Roman historian Suetonius, when Augustus heard the news of the defeat "he was so greatly affected that for several months in succession he cut neither his beard nor his hair, and sometimes he would dash his head against a door, crying: "Quintilius Varus, give me back my legions!" He observed the day of the disaster each year as one of sorrow and mourning. (Suetonius, *Augustus* 23.2)

24 More than thirty years later: Jerome, *De Virus Illustribus* (PL 23, 646). Gischala, today known as Jish, was a Jewish town just twenty-five miles north of Nazareth, often mentioned by Josephus: *Jewish War* 2.575, 585, 621, 629, 632. Apparently, the author of the book of Acts did not know this background of Paul. In one of the speeches he composed for Paul, he has him claiming that he was "born" in Tarsus of Cilicia, which would not technically be correct (Acts 22:3; cf. 21:8, which just says he was "brought up" in Tarsus). Regarding Paul's visit to James, who lived with Mary and the other brothers in Jerusalem after Jesus's crucifixion, see Galatians 1:8, 2:9; Acts 15:13, 12:17. See Todd Penner, "Paul and Roman Citizenship," Bible Odyssey, [n.d.], bibleodyssey.org.

26 The clear intent was to ensure: Tabor, "Crucifixion: 'That Most Wretched of Deaths' What Do We Know?," Taborblog, September 17, 2017, jamestabor.com.

27 The Romans responded with full force: Josephus, *Jewish War* 2.57–59.

28 This text refers to a "Messiah": See Ethan Bronner, "Ancient Tablet Excites Debate on Messiah and Resurrection," *New York Times*, July 6, 2008; and for an evaluation of the tablet and its textual details, see Israel Knohl, "The Messiah Son of David: 'Gabriel's Revelation' and the Birth of a New Messianic Model," *Biblical Archaeology Review* (September/October 2008): 58–62.

28 Athrongaeus and his brothers: Josephus, *Jewish War* 2.60–65.

CHAPTER THREE: THE FORGOTTEN CITY OF SEPPHORIS

30 Tradition has it that: See Ward, "Sepphoris," 396–397, and Folda, "The Church of Saint Anne."

30 It was there where she would have been born: This idea that Mary grew up in Jerusalem and was given over to the priests at age three and lived in the temple like a vestal virgin, fed by angels, is late and legendary, based on the so-called Protoevangelium of James. This text is often dated to the late second century, but there is no certain evidence for its existence until the early third century, when the Christian writer Origen first mentions the text, saying it is of dubious origin and recent appearance. A third-century Greek

copy, the Bodmer Papyrus, was recently discovered. The work is known by several names: most commonly the Protoevangelium of James but also the Gospel of James, the Infancy Gospel of James, the Birth of Mary, the Story of the Birth of Saint Mary Mother of God, and the Revelation of James. To avoid confusion, I will stay with the rather unwieldy Protoevangelium of James. Mary's parents, Joachim and Anna, are not named in the New Testament, but do appear in this text; see Hennecke and Schneemelcher, vol. I, 421–37, as well as the more modern translation by Ronald F. Hock, *The Infancy Gospels.* Joachim and Anna became popular figures in Catholic lore, and their story was a favorite theme of Renaissance artists. Churches were dedicated to St. Anne as early as the fifth century and are common throughout the world today, including the famous Church of St. Anne in the Old City of Jerusalem near the Lion's Gate.

31 It is first mentioned by: Origen's Commentary on Matthew 10.17 in *The Ante-Nicene Fathers,* vol. 2: "But some say, basing it on a tradition in the Gospel according to Peter, as it is entitled, or 'The Book of James' [i.e., the Protoevangelium of James] that the brethren of Jesus were sons of Joseph by a former wife, whom he married before Mary. Now those who say so wish to preserve the honour of Mary in virginity to the end, so that that body of hers which was appointed to minister to the Word which said, 'The Holy Ghost shall come upon thee and the power of the Most High shall overshadow thee,' might not know intercourse with a man after that the Holy Ghost came into her and the power from on high overshadowed her."

31 It first appears in this: Pelikan, *Mary Through the Centuries,* 55–65.

32 Many of the places he visits: The anonymous Bordeaux Pilgrim is our earliest pilgrim account, dating to AD 333–334, followed by that of Egeria, a Christian woman who wrote a detailed account of her pilgrimage to the Holy Land dated c. AD 380. We also have the records of the fourth-century Christian historian Eusebius as well as Socrates, who supplements Eusebius's work in the fifth century with references to the emperor Constantine's mother, Helena, who built churches to mark various sites related to early Christian tradition. See Finegan, *Archaeology of the New Testament,* 65.

35 The Via Maris: See Trevor Harris, *Proving Biblical Nazareth: Evidence for the Key Sites of Jesus* (Norwood, South Australia: Key-line Christian Research, 2017), 3–34.

37 Even though the house is long gone: See Dark, "Has Jesus' Nazareth House Been Found?" and "Early Roman-Period Nazareth and the Sisters of Nazareth Covenant." See also Dark's more official reports: *Sepphoris-Nazareth Survey* as well as his updated general overview in *Archaeology of Jesus' Nazareth* (Oxford University Press, 2023). In the latter Dark carefully evaluates all the archaeological evidence, pro and con, that leads him to

date these structures to the time of Mary and Jesus. For an overview and bibliography of archaeological evidence related to Nazareth, with differing interpretations, see Gregory C. Jenks, "The Quest for the Historical Nazareth," in *Bethsaida in Archaeology, History and Ancient Culture: A Festschrift in Honor of John T. Greene*, edited by J. Harold Ellens (Newcastle upon Tyne: Cambridge Scholars Publishing, 2014).

37 Israeli archaeologists uncovered: See Owen Jarus, "Jesus' House? 1st-Century Structure May Be Where He Grew Up," LiveScience, March 1, 2015, livescience.com.

38 His aristocratic tastes: Josephus, *Jewish Antiquities* 18.27.

39 Its water supply: For a comprehensive archaeological survey with drawings and illustrations see James F. Strange, "Sepphoris: The Jewel of the Galilee," in David A. Fiensy and James Riley Strange, eds. *Galilee in the Late Second Temple and Mishnaic Periods: The Archaeological Record from Cities, Towns, and Villages*, vol. 2 (Minneapolis: Fortress Press, 2014).

44 Maccabee means "hammer": According to Josephus, who was also of the priestly Hasmonean family, Asmoneus was the great-grandfather of Mattathias, the father of the five Maccabean sons. "Maccabee" is more of a nickname, meaning "hammer"; see Josephus, *Life* 1–2.

44 Maccabean coins were popular: Danny Syon has investigated everyday "small change" coinage in Galilee based on archaeological finds over the past few decades. His remarkable results show the predominance of Hasmonean coins in the region during Mary's time. See his *Small Change in Hellenistic-Roman Galilee*.

45 By choosing those names: We have a good handle on the frequency of Jewish names in this period in the land of Israel from careful tallies that have been done on ossuary inscriptions and in contemporary literary accounts. Regarding these names we can estimate the following percentages of known names of individuals in the period: Simon (16 percent), Judas (15 percent), Salome (25 percent), and Mariam/Mary (20 percent). See Hachlili, *Jewish Funerary Customs*, 196–200, and individual entries in Ilan, *Lexicon of Jewish Names*.

CHAPTER FOUR: GAME OF THRONES

47 Mary's genealogical record: I will offer my reasons for thinking the genealogy of Luke 3:23–28 is that of Mary, and not of Joseph, subsequently. At this point I just want to offer context for understanding her life under the rule of Herod the Great.

48 A final handful of 960: For a general account of what happened at Masada in this final act of defiance, see Tabor, "Acquiring Life in a Single Moment," in Droge and Tabor, *A Noble Death*. On the archaeological evaluation of the

Notes

human remains dated to that period found in excavations in 1963–1965, see Tabor, "Masada Mysteries: What Do We Know About the Bones?," Taborblog, July 2, 2016, jamestabor.com.

51 First, he says that what most inspired: Josephus, *Jewish War* 6.312. The oracle is most likely the prophecy of Daniel 9:24–27, which specifies a period of "Seventy Weeks of Years"—that is, 490 years—until the coming of an anointed "Prince" who would bring to fulfillment the eschatological prophecies.

51 Second, he tells us that Herod the Great: Josephus, *Jewish War* 7.300–303.

52 Few are aware: Unless otherwise indicated all of the information about Herod the Great and the events surrounding his life are taken from the first-century Jewish historian Josephus, our main primary source. I will not reference every event mentioned here to the writings of Josephus, since readers can consult *Jewish Antiquities*, books 14–16, and *Jewish War*, book I; see also the Flavius Josephus Primer Home Page, josephus.org. My teacher Louis H. Feldman, perhaps the most revered Josephus scholar of his generation, once made the statement that there is no figure of the ancient world whom we know more about than Herod the Great. See Feldman's "Josephus" in *The Anchor Bible Dictionary* and his *Josephus and Modern Scholarship*. The accounts we have of Herod in Josephus's *Jewish Antiquities* and *Jewish War* are often contradictory and often imaginative. Josephus has his sources, but he also, like all authors, slants his portrayals according to his sympathies, with his imperial patrons always in mind. One of the best comprehensive critical historical resources on Herod is Peter Richardson's *Herod: King of the Jews*. See also Samuel Sandmel, *Herod: Profile of a Tyrant* and L. I. Levine's "Herod the Great" in *The Anchor Bible Dictionary*.

53 Herod's father, Antipater: The influential and wealthy Antipater was by birth an Idumean, a tribe that lived to the south of the Dead Sea in the northern Negev Desert. Josephus says that the Hasmonean king John Hyrcanus (who reigned 135–104 BC) conquered them and forced their nominal conversion to Judaism. This view has been challenged by Aryeh Kasher, who claims the evidence shows that the conversion of the Idumeans was peaceful and voluntary; see the discussion in Richardson, *Herod*, 55–62, which questions Josephus's assertion of forced conversion.

53 Josephus describes Herod: Josephus, *Jewish War* 1.13.

54 Herod fell hopelessly in love: Her name is spelled Μαριάμη/Mariam. The name comes from the Hebrew Bible, where it is first used for Miriam, the sister of Moses and Aaron (Exodus 15:20). Some English translations of Josephus double the second *m*, so one gets Mariamme. Still later, one finds translations adding the letter *nun* or *n*, so you find Mariamne.

54 Doris was from a Jewish family: *Jewish War* 1.241, 432–443.

54 It should be noted that: Luke prefers the name Mariam, which is closer to

177

the Hebrew, and he uses it almost exclusively for Jesus's mother, instead of the Greek form Maria (Μαρία)—which is closer to our English "Mary" (see Luke 1:27, 30, 34, 38–39, 46, 56; 2:5, 16, 19, 34; Acts 1:14). On the variations of the name Mary in Hebrew, Aramaic, and Greek, see Tal Ilan, *Lexicon of Jewish Names*, 242–244.

55 This possibility is supported by: The Babylonian Talmud, tractate *Sanhedrin* 106b.

59 Hyrcanus had ruled: Josephus, *Jewish War* 1.68. Josephus writes that Hyrcanus was esteemed by God and the "only man to have all three of the most desirable things: ruler of the nation, the high priesthood, and the gift of prophecy."

59 His monumental tomb: See Josephus, *Jewish War* 1.54–69 for an account of his illustrious reign. His tomb is mentioned frequently by Josephus, see *Jewish War* 5.259, 304, 356; 6.169.

59 The Romans desecrated it: Ironically, today it is the location of the holiest site in Christendom, the Church of the Holy Sepulchre, which millions revere as the place of Jesus's crucifixion and resurrection. This location was not identified as the place of the crucifixion until the early fourth century, during the reign of the emperor Constantine, three hundred years *after* the time of Jesus, though it has the support of many scholars and archaeologists. A more likely location is the Mount of Olives; see my study "Locating Golgotha," Taborblog, February 6, 2016, jamestabor.com.

59 Also, the enemies of Hyrcanus: Certain Pharisees, who opposed the Hasmoneans at one point, cast doubts on the purity of his lineage owing to his mother being held captive by Antiochus Epiphanes, the tyrant who sparked the Maccabean revolt in 165 BC. The implication was that she very well might have been raped, meaning that Hyrcanus would not even have a Jewish father. A similar accusation surfaced against Hyrcanus's son Alexander Jannaeus—that his grandmother might have been raped.

CHAPTER FIVE: THAT OTHER KING OF THE JEWS

63 As Herod conducted his cleanup campaign: Josephus, *Jewish War* 1.309–313.

67 It is written in the first person: See "Cold Case: Did Archaeologists Find the last Maccabean King, After All?," *Haaretz*, April 29, 2014, haaretz.com, as well as my blog post "The Abba Cave, Crucifixion Nails, and the Last Hasmonean King," Taborblog, April 3, 2016, jamestabor.com. For a skeptical counterview and an extensive bibliography, see "The Abba Inscription," in Hannah M. Cotton et al., *Corpus Inscriptionum Iudaeae/Palaestinae*, vol. I: *Jerusalem*, part I:1–704 (Berlin: De Gruyter, 2010), 98–101.

67 At first, the skeleton was identified: Despite recent naysaying by those

who are apparently not aware of all the facts, see Joe Zias, "A Jerusalem tomb, 'blind leading the blind' or just another Day in Paradise?," The Bible and Interpretation, April 2014, bibleinterp.arizona.edu. The case that the tomb held the remains of a crucified/beheaded male, as Nicu Haas, the anthropologist who first examined it, asserted, seems likely. This is further supported by the latest analysis from Prof. Hershkovitz. Those who have argued that crucifixion nails went through the wrist, not the hands, and that these nails are too "short" to be for crucifixion, are just mistaken. Hershkovitz has definitely clarified this issue. The nails are driven into the palm, then either angled or bent into a hook, not to hold up the body but to keep the hands and arms in place, which were supported by ropes—thus "tacking" or pinning the hands to the wood behind. The hypothesis that this individual was the Hasmonean royal priest/king Antigonus turns out to be a live option.

67　In 2016, I was invited to participate: See the program *Last Days of Jesus*, PBS, pbs.org.

67　As part of that research: She is mentioned a half-dozen times in Josephus, but always as the unnamed wife—or widow—of his father, Aristobulus. We know she bore him four children, two boys, Alexander and Antigonus, and two daughters.

67　Since Jewish priests: I am publishing those results here for the first time, with plans for more such DNA tests in the future. It is one thing to study texts, or even dig up artifacts; but through the miracle of our new methods of recovering even ancient DNA, an entirely new historical avenue of investigation is opening. So far as I know, the team I am working with is the first to ever work with ancient DNA from Jerusalem from the time of the Herods. The potential implications are a bit overwhelming to contemplate. Preliminary work on the residue inside several ossuaries from the period are showing promise of solid DNA test results. The polymorphisms are highlighted in the chart below. These results are from mtDNA Haplogroup K and very strongly associated with the subclade of K1a1b1a. This subclade is commonly found in modern Jewish groups, particularly the Ashkenazi Jews, but rarely found in non-Jewish groups. Some have further associated this subclade with modern-day Jews who have Kohanim, or priestly, ancestry; see Behar et al., "The Matrilineal Ancestry of Ashkenazi Jewry."

Polymorphisms HV1 and HV2

(1)	(2)	(3)	(4)
Position	Standard RCRS	Sample 1	Revised Sample 2
16224	T	C	C
16234	C	T	T
16290	C	C	C
16294	C	Y	C
16311	T	Y	C
16355	C	C	C
73	A	G	G
114	C	T	T
263	A	G	G
315.1	–	C	C

67 Despite Herod's consolidation of power: Historians know Jonathan by his more official title, Aristobulus III. Josephus relates Herod's murder of Jonathan and the surrounding events in a long, detailed passage in *Jewish Antiquities*, 15.23–76, with a shorter parallel account in *Jewish War*, 1.435–444.

68 Alexandra, elated at the idea: Josephus relates this extended tale in *Jewish Antiquities*, 15.23–87, with a shorter version in *Jewish War*, 1.431–444.

72 I had visited the ancient town: The site is known today as Tulul Abu al-'Alayiq. In 1950 an ASOR expedition initiated more scientific excavating. See James L. Kelso, "New Testament Jericho," *The Biblical Archaeologist* 14, no. 2 (1951): 34–43 for the preliminary excavations done in 1950. Ehud Netzer excavated ten seasons beginning in 1973; see Netzer, Rachel Bar-Nathan, et al., *Hasmonean and Herodian Palaces at Jericho: Final Reports of the 1973–1987 Excavations* (Jerusalem: Israel Exploration Society, 2001). At the Hasmonean level, Netzer discovered a massive limestone plastered pool more than 100 by 60 feet in size and 12 feet deep. It is divided into two parts by a partition about 18 feet wide, half the depth of the pool. Broad steps lead to the bottom of each half of the pool. Alongside is a sizable poolside pavilion built at the same time as the pool. This is most likely the pool in which Jonathan was drowned.

72 The Hasmoñeans had initially built a palace: Josephus, *Jewish Antiquities* 1.407.

72 Their grandfather, the high priest Aristobulus: Josephus, *Jewish Antiquities* 14.123; *Jewish War* 1.183.

73 As the years passed: Josephus, *Jewish Antiquities* 15.218–231.

74 He began to neglect: Josephus, *Jewish Antiquities* 15.240–246.

75 Besides Doris and Mariame: Doris (Antipater); Mariame I (Alexander,

Aristobulus, Salampsio, Cypros); Mariame II (Herod II); Malthace (Archelaus, Antipas, Olympias); Cleopatra of Jerusalem (Philip, unnamed son); Pallas (Phasael); Phaidra (Roxanne); Elpis (Salome); two wives who were cousins with no known children.

76 Herod became bitterly envious: *Jewish Antiquities* 17.92; *Jewish War* 1.565.

76 Toward the end, his only relief: *Jewish War* 1.656.

76 Reportedly, the emperor Augustus: Macrobius, *Saturnalia* 2:4:11.

CHAPTER SIX: MARY'S SECRET

79 The long list includes: For some samples of such tales see my compilation "Divine Men, Heroes, and Gods," jamestabor.com; as well as Talbert, "Miraculous Conceptions and Births." For comparisons to the kind of tales that develop around Jesus, see Morton Smith, "Prolegomena to a Discussion of Aretalogies, Divine Men, the Gospels and Jesus," *Journal of Biblical Literature* 90, no. 2 (1971): 174–199.

79 The ancient world did not share: See the insightful summary of ancient evidence, including that of our New Testament Gospels, by Andrew Lincoln, "How Babies Were Made in Jesus' Time," *Biblical Archaeology Review* 40, no. 6 (Nov./Dec. 2014): 42–49.

80 And yet, we find hints: In the fourth-century apocryphal text called the Acts of Pilate, which relates an account of Jesus's trial before the Roman prefect Pontius Pilate, one of the charges made by Jesus's enemies echoes the text in John—namely, "You were born of fornication." No one takes this text as an accurate account of the trial of Jesus; it is wholly legendary, but it shows that the slander persisted over time. (Acts of Pilate 2.3) See J. K. Elliott, ed., *The Apocryphal New Testament: A Collection of Apocryphal Christian Literature in an English Translation Based on M. R. James* (Oxford: Clarendon Press, 1993), 172–173.

81 They also call Jesus a "Samaritan": The Samaritans claimed to be remnants of the northern tribes of Israel—sometimes referred to as the "Lost Tribes"—who remained in the land after the Assyrian captivity in the eighth century BC. They were generally considered by the Jews in the time of Jesus as a mixed race whose ancestry could not be verified. The two charges are thus related—being of illegitimate birth and having a Samaritan father with no established pedigree. Herod the Great had ten wives but one of them, Malthace, was a Samaritan. She was the mother of Herod Antipas and Archelaus, his two most prominent surviving sons, whom the emperor Augustus appointed over Galilee and Judea, respectively. Herod and his son Antipas desperately sought some kind of legitimization of their lineages through marriages to women with priestly pedigrees. Josephus, *Jewish War* 1.562.

81 The second-century AD Christian writer: Tertullian, *De Spectaculis* 30.
This is my translation of the Latin "Hic est ille, dicam, fabri aut quaestu-
ariae filius, sabbati destructor, Samarites et daemonium habens."

81 Each of the four: Tamar posed as a prostitute and got pregnant by Judah,
son of Jacob (Genesis 38); Rahab was the prostitute that aided the Israelite spies in conquering Jericho (Joshua 6); Ruth was a Moabite woman
who crawled into bed with Boaz—grandfather of King David (Ruth 3);
and Bathsheba, mother of Solomon and Nathan, committed adultery with
King David (2 Samuel 11).

82 Saying 105 is the most interesting: Gospel of Thomas translation in Hennecke and Schneemelcher, eds., *New Testament Apocrypha*, vol. I, 511–522.

82 This can also be translated: Some have interpreted the saying as a reference to the Gnostic notion of despising physical birth—i.e., "hating one's
mother and father"—but in that case one would more likely be called an
"orphan" rather than "son of a harlot," the precise charge circulating about
Jesus's birth. Robert Funk, who reflects the majority opinion of the Jesus
Seminar Fellows, asserts that this saying has to do with disputes with rival
Judean groups over Jesus's legitimacy; see Funk and Hover, *The Five Gospels*,
526.

82 The Jewish term for a child born: See Bruce Chilton, *Rabbi Jesus*, 5–22, as
well as his online article "The Mamzer Jesus and His Birth," bibleinterp
.arizona.edu.

82 There is also the term "foundling": These categories are laid out in the
Mishnah, Kiddushin 4: priests, Israelites, impaired priests, converts, freed
slaves, mamzers, temple servants (*netinim*), hushlings, and foundlings. Such
categories are primarily about who can verifiably establish lineage and who
can rightfully marry whom. What we don't know is to what extent people
in fact formed their social groups and boundaries around such distinctions
in Mary's time. As in any age, religious authorities often legislate and make
their demands, only to be ignored by both rulers and commoners. We
don't want to make the mistake of reading rabbinic imagination from later
centuries back into life in Galilee in the first century.

82 The Jewish Mishnah: Yebamot 4:13; see under "Jesus" in *The Jewish Ency-
clopedia*, 170, for further comment on this passage. See also Schäfer, *Jesus
in the Talmud*, 15–24. Tales of Mary's adultery and Jesus's illegitimacy run
through many later rabbinic texts.

82 The term "such-a-one": The first-century rabbi Elisha ben Abuyah was
regularly called "Acher," meaning "the Other," to avoid using his name.
Compare *Yoma* 66a.

82 There is an oblique reference: b. Sanhedrin 106a.

83 This persistent theme: See Schäfer, *Jesus in the Talmud*, 15–24 and 97–102,

for an analysis of the basic references, but compare Klausner, *Jesus of Naza-reth*, and Krauss, *Das Leben Jesu.*

84 It was first suggested: I thank my graduate student Chad Day for first pointing out to me the origin and/or promotion of this idea in Nitzsch, "Über eine Reihe talmudischer." Joseph Klausner (1874–1958) was a Jew-ish historian and professor of Hebrew literature at the Hebrew Univer-sity of Jerusalem. In 1922, he published his study of the life of Jesus in Hebrew, *Yeshu Ha-Notzri* (Jerusalem: Shtibel, 1922). It was translated into English by Herbert Danby as *Jesus of Nazareth: His Life, Times, and Teaching* (London: Allen and Unwin, 1925). Although some scholars doubted the explanation on philological grounds—*parthenos* and *pantera* are not closely homophonic—it was repeated endlessly, with no serious investigation, until it achieved the status of a scholarly *imprimatur*. See, for example, Rob-ert E. Van Voorst, *Jesus Outside the New Testament: An Introduction to the Ancient Evidence* (Grand Rapids, MI: Eerdmans, 2000), 117. Even John P. Meier, whose research on Jesus tends to be one of the most thorough in terms of evaluating sources, relying upon Klausner, seems to accept this explanation of the "name" Pantera; see *A Marginal Jew*, 96.

85 In another example: James in English = Jacob in Hebrew. It is possible that the name Sikhnin is confused for Shikin, as we know it today, a Jewish village clustered around Sepphoris—just a mile to the northwest. The site is currently being excavated by James Strange from Samford University. Eliezar became one of the greatest rabbis of his time, but he was likely edu-cated as a Pharisee before the horrible days of the destruction of Jerusalem in AD 70 and its aftermath, when most of the leading Jerusalem Pharisees fled north to Sepphoris in Galilee. It is not historically impossible that this Jacob could be "James the brother of Jesus." The identification with Jesus's brother was suggested by Klausner in *Jesus of Nazareth*, 41–42. See the discussion of Richard Bauckham in *Jude and the Relatives of Jesus*, 106–121. Bauckham does not categorically reject the identification with Jesus's brother James, though he suggests a more likely choice, chronologically, would be another James, the grandson (or some say son) of Jude, who was the brother of Jesus.

85 The answer pleased Eliezar: The three texts are: t. Hullin 2:24; Kohelet Rabbah 1:8:3; *b.'Abodah Zarah* 16b–17a. In this case the later text, from the Babylonian Talmud, also substitutes "Jesus the Nazarene" for "Jesus son of Pantera."

86 The various sects of Judaism: See Cohen, *From the Maccabees to the Mishnah* and *The Beginnings of Jewishness.*

86 These earliest references to Pantera: Peter Schäfer's *Jesus in the Talmud* is the best study of these later materials. Without claiming they give us accurate

historical information, Schäfer shows that such references, even though often cryptic, do in fact refer to Jesus of Nazareth. This is in sharp contrast to Johann Maier, who denies there are any significant references to Jesus in the rabbinic literature; see his magnum opus *Jesus von Nazareth in der talmudischen Überlieferung* (Darmstadt: Wissenschaftliche Buchgesellschaft, 1978). The tradition carries well into the Middle Ages, with the polemical Jewish treatise known as *Toledot Yeshu*, which exists in many versions: see Krauss, *Das Leben Jesu*, who includes nine different versions of the text. Many of the English translations omit the "seduction scene" as too offensive.

86 These earliest references: What survives is a detailed refutation by the early third-century Christian apologist Origen, titled *Against Celsus*. In refuting Celsus's arguments, Origen quotes his entire work, paragraph by paragraph, and then adds his responses bit by bit. By collecting all these quotations, and assembling them, scholars have been able to reconstruct Celsus's original work.

86 Let us imagine what a Jew: Imaginative reconstruction based on *Contra Celsius* I.28; see Henry Chadwick (Cambridge University Press, 2003) for original text of Origen.

87 Epiphanius, an early-fourth-century Christian writer: Epiphanius, *The Panarion, De Fide* II and III 78:7–5 through 8:2.

87 John of Damascus: John of Damascus, *De Fid. Orthod.* iv, 14. See the theologian Andrew of Crete (*Patrologia Graeca* 97.916) and a later Byzantine monk named Epiphanius (*Patrologia Graeca* 120.190).

88 He writes that she is: *Doctrina Jacobi* V.16, 209. See *Doctrina Jacobi nuper Baptizati*, in G. Dagron and V. Déroche, "Juifs et Chrétiens dans l'Orient du VIIe siècle," *Travaux et Mémoires* 11 (1991): 17–248, which contains an edition of the Greek text with French translation.

88 There is a first-century Jewish tomb: [ιω]σηπου πενθερου [δρ]οσου. See Clermont-Ganneau, "Notes on Hebrew and Jewish Inscriptions," *Palestine Exploration Fund Quarterly Statement* 23 (1891): 242–243). The ossuary is not part of the Israel State Collection and does not appear to be included in *Corpus Inscriptionum Iudaeae/Palesestinae*, vol. I, part I (2010), though it is included in *Corpus Inscriptionum Judaicarum* no, 1211. The inscription itself was based on a squeeze in the possession of Clermont-Ganneau. I am told that most of Clermont-Ganneau's inscriptions were sent to either the Palestine Exploration Fund in London or the Louvre in Paris. Clermont-Ganneau took the middle "name" to be a family designation for father-in-law, or son-in-law, or brother-in-law, and thus read it as "Of Joseph, father-in-law of Drosus," taking the third name as an ordinary transcription of the common Roman name *Drusus*, adopted by Jews in the period (see Josephus, *Jewish Antiquities* 18.132; אורד ,הסורד *y. Yoma* 4: 41d; *y. Shabbat* I: 4a). Tal Ilan (*Lexicon of Jewish Names*, 301) disagrees. She reads

πενθερος as the only example we have found in Palestine of the Greek name Pentheros = Panthera, otherwise found in Latin inscriptions and Greek and Aramaic sources, some of which give it as the name for the father of Jesus.

88 Outside Israel, the name Pantera: Deissmann, *Light from the Ancient East*, 73–75. Deissmann published a more extensive treatment in his 1906 article "Der Name Panthera." He gives a half dozen examples of the name Pantera published in *Corpus Inscriptionum Latinarum*, the comprehensive multivolume collection of Latin inscriptions from the Roman world—including the Bingerbrück tombstone of the Sidonian archer. See also the summary of Patterson, "Origin of the Name Pantera."

90 Whether he was Jewish: The best and most recent study is by Zeichmann, "Jesus 'ben Pantera'." His insightful analysis of all the issues related to what we might be able to responsibly say about this Roman soldier, his names, and his forty years of service, are most helpful.

90 Some have proposed: See Schaberg, *The Illegitimacy of Jesus*. For reactions see her prologue, "Feminism Lashes Back: Responses to the Backlash," 3–10.

91 It is possible: See Josephus, *Jewish Antiquities* 12.257–260.

91 This fact alone: Zeichmann, "Jesus 'ben Pantera'," 153.

94 Serapion, a fourth-century bishop: Serapion, *Life of John the Baptizer* 3:9–15. See Slavomir Čéplö "The Life of John the Baptist by Serapion," 268–292.

94 From Nazareth, this hundred-mile journey: I have come to know the area well. I've spent five years excavating a nearby cave at a hill called Suba that we refer to as "the John the Baptizer cave," a water reservoir carved out of bedrock and fed by a natural spring. It is mentioned in our ancient sources as the hiding place of Elizabeth and the baby John when she fled from Herod the Great, shortly after the birth of Jesus. See Gibson, *The Cave of John the Baptist.*

95 Serapion also relates: Serapion, *Life of John the Baptizer,* 6:10.

CHAPTER SEVEN: DOUBLY ROYAL

97 The surprise is: Names such as Mattatha, Matthat (twice), Levi (twice), Eliezar, Mattathias (twice), and Jannai (Janaeus) are distinctively priestly, favored by the Hasmoneans.

98 The Bible offers dozens: Genesis 5, 10; I Chronicles 1–8.

99 Since these two grandfathers: Since the third century, various early Christian writers have devised an ingenious but convoluted explanation based on what is called levirate marriage—from the Latin *levir*, meaning "husband's brother." The Torah provides that if a married man dies childless, his brother can take his widow as wife, and the first son born will be legally registered as the heir of the dead brother, thus preserving his inheritance

(Deuteronomy 25:5–6; compare Mark 12:18–23). This meant that a man could technically have two fathers—one legal, the other biological. The assumption then is that the two grandfathers, Jacob and Heli, were brothers, and one or the other died, so that either of them can be said to be Joseph's father—one biological and the other adoptive. Our earliest church historian, Eusebius (*Church History* 1.7.16), attributes this view to Julius Africanus, who argued that Joseph was legally the son of Eli (Luke) but physically the son of Jacob (Matthew)—two brothers. Matthan of the line of Solomon begat Jacob, then died, and Melchi of the line of Nathan begat Eli from the same mother—Estha. As a result, Eli and Jacob were only half brothers. When Eli died without children, Jacob raised up seed from him, begetting Joseph as his own son but the legal son of Eli. See Raymond Brown, *The Birth of the Messiah*, 503–504, for an analysis and discussion.

99 Eli is another form of the name: Just as Eliakim and Jehoakim are the names of son of Josiah, king of Judah in the sixth century BC (2 Kings 23:34; 2 Chronicles 36:4).

99 Many scholars have dismissed: See the exhaustive analysis and extensive bibliography of Brown, *The Birth of the Messiah*, 55–95. Brown rejects the idea that Luke is giving Mary's genealogy, though he discusses the pros and cons.

100 Though commonly repeated: See Marcus J. Borg and John Dominic Crossan, *The First Christmas: What the Gospels Really Teach About Jesus's Birth* (San Francisco: HarperCollins, 2009).

100 Herod appointed undeserving men: *Jewish Antiquities* 20.247–248. Josephus, born in AD 37, proudly traced his own ancestry back to these distinguished Hasmoneans, through his great-great-grandfather Matthias, who married a daughter of Jonathan the Maccabee. His father, also named Matthias, married a woman of Hasmonean ancestry. As a result, he could claim this pedigree from both sides of his family.

101 Herod's own ancestry: This report circulates among early Christians; see Africanus, Epistle to Aristides, cited by Eusebius, *Church History* 1.7.11–13.

101 Africanus . . . says that Herod ordered: Our source for Julius Africanus is Eusebius in his *Church History*, 1.7.13. Some have doubted the veracity of this report since Josephus claims his own pedigree as a Hasmonean priest is preserved in the public registers, but his birth is over a hundred years after the beginning of Herod's reign, and Sepphoris, destroyed in 4 BC and then rebuilt by Herod Antipas as his magnificent capital, would have certainly once again contained such archives (*Life* 3–6; cf. *Against Apion* I, 30–32).

101 Josephus tells us: *Life* 38–39.

102 We also have references: According to Rabbi Yose ben Halafta, who was born in Sepphoris; see Qiddushin 4. There is a passage in the Jerusalem Talmud that preserves Rabbi Yose's genealogy; see y. Ta'anit 4.2; cf. Genesis Rabba 98:13.

102 Africanus wrote: Quoted by Eusebius, *Church History* 1.7.13–14. Africanus is best known for his work *Chronographiae*, a five-volume chronology that attempted to chart human history from creation to his own time, approximately AD 221. Unfortunately, it survives only in fragments in quotations of other historians and writers such as Eusebius and Origen.

102 In the case of Mary: See the extensive work on the *desposuni* in Bauckham, *Jude and the Relatives of Jesus.*

102 "The Lukan genealogy": See Bauckham, "The Lukan Genealogy of Jesus," in *Jude and the Relatives of Jesus*, 315–372. His arguments for the historical value of Luke's genealogy are persuasive, though as far as I can determine he does not go on to claim that this is the genealogy of Mary.

103 Since he is not focused: In one of the later New Testament letters attributed to Paul, the author laments Jewish groups that occupy themselves with "endless genealogies" rather than relying upon their "faith" to connect them to Abraham (I Timothy 1:4; Galatians 3:29). Such a protest is not made in a vacuum. It is clearly directed against other followers of Jesus, most likely those who were connected to the Jewish origins of the emerging Christian faith—followers of James the brother of Jesus in particular, who did consider such matters of pedigree essential to the core idea of messianism. Paul refers to James in a dismissive way, although he is clearly the most authoritative figure in the early church—even above Peter and John. We must remember that Paul never met Jesus. He was a latecomer to the movement. Paul plainly says that he values his own visionary and clairvoyant revelations above the one-on-one experiences of these original followers directly with Jesus (Galatians 1:11–17). Paul refers to them as the "so-called Pillars of the Church," but then adds, "what they are means nothing to me" (Galatians 2:19).

While Paul grudging grants that Jesus was descended from King David "according to the flesh," he was not interested in the human Jesus, but rather in the heavenly Christ (Romans 1:3). He states unequivocally that he no longer regards Jesus "according to the flesh" as having any importance (2 Corinthians 5:16). The phrase in Greek might be paraphrased as: "We no longer look at Jesus as a human being, born of a woman, but as the heavenly glorified Christ."

In Paul's view, pedigree and matters of ancestry became meaningless. Paul would no doubt have had the same attitude toward Mary. While she might be the *mortal* mother of Jesus, he writes that the heavenly Jerusalem now is the "mother of us all" (Galatians 5:26). Paul is interested in a new spiritual family that is determined not by what he calls "flesh and blood," but by the new birth of the Spirit.

104 Similarly, only those of the direct lineage: Later, when the country was divided by a civil war in the eighth century BC, this same Davidic line continued to rule as kings over the southern kingdom of Judah. When Jerusalem was destroyed by the Babylonians in 586 BC, there were no further kings of Israel. The royal line of David was cut off. But the Hebrew prophets foretold an ideal future in which God would raise up from the "seed" of David a king or messiah who would eventually rule the entire world in peace and justice (Isaiah 11).

104 Neither the Persians: In contrast, Cyrus, the king of Persia, who had conquered Babylon, allowed Jews to return to their land and to rebuild their nation seventy years after their captivity. Cyrus even allowed them to reinstate their Aaronic line of priests. We read about this in the book of Zechariah, now part of the Hebrew Bible. A priest named Joshua was first to so serve, and we can trace his priestly lineage down through the Hasmoneans, which brings us to Mary's time. It was his "anointing" as high priest that restored the priesthood and was seen as a herald of the one to come—namely, the "Branch" of David, or the king messiah (Zechariah 3:1–10).

104 Josephus says that John Hyrcanus: *Jewish Antiquities* 13.299; *Jewish War* 1.68.

104 He was succeeded by: Josephus, *Jewish Antiquities* 13.301–315; *Jewish War* 1.85–106.

104 The ancient Greek geographer: *Geographica*. XVI.2.40.

105 What stands out is: These overstruck coins have the obverse bearing the lily model and the paleo-Hebrew inscription "Yehonatan the King" and have on its reverse the symbol of the anchor with the Greek inscription "of King Alexander." Over the original coin exists an overstriking that contains the minting of the priestly die of a double cornucopia with the staff and pomegranate and on its other side the Paleo-Hebrew inscription. Sometimes the inscription shown is "Yntn the High Priest and the Council of the Jews," and sometimes it is difficult to distinguish the name in the inscription.

105 He is called a "furious young Lion": 1Q169 (*4QNahum Pesher*) frags. 3-4, col. I.7. English translation is mine.

106 At Jannaeus's death: There had only been one previous Jewish queen, Athaliah, the mother of the ninth-century Israelite king Ahaziah, who attempted a short-lived coup after her son's death, killing other heirs of the throne of David and installing herself as queen for six years (2 Kings 11:1–16).

106 While she has often been called: 4Q322, fr. 2.

106 According to Josephus: She died mysteriously of a "serious illness," much before her time, resulting in the political rivalry for power that would only be resolved by the Romans in appointing Herod king of the Jews; *Jewish Antiquities* 13.422–432.

109 It also says in the New Testament: See Peter Willem van der Horst, "Did Sarah Have a Seminal Emission?," *Bible Review* 8.1 (Feb. 1992): 34–39.

109 He writes that Jesus: See William Adler, "Exodus 6:23 and the High Priest from the Tribe of Judah," *Journal of Theological Studies* 48, no. 1 (1997): 24–47.

109 Hegesippus, a second-century Jewish convert: Eusebius, *Church History* 2.23.4–6.

109 According to Epiphanius: Epiphanius, *Panarion* 29.4.2–4.

110 It relates that Mary: See Adler, "On the Priesthood of Jesus."

110 We even have one text: *The Second Apocalypse of James* 50:18–22. See James M. Robinson, *The Nag Hammadi Library*, 271.

111 Her monumental work: Ilan, *Lexicon of Jewish Names in Late Antiquity*. See also Ilan, "'Man Born of Woman . . .'"

111 It is rather striking: See references to Joseph and/or Jesus's "father" in Luke 2:48, 3:23, 4:22; Matthew 13:55; and John 1:45, 6:42.

112 Both posed the same threat: Josephus, *Antiquities* 18.118.

112 In Mark: The common Christian translation "You are a priest after the order of Melchizedek" is misleading, since the proper name Melchizedek means "king of righteousness." The Hebrew is clear—one addressed as a "king of righteousness" is declared to be a priest forever, according to God's decree (see Jewish Publication Society translation). Later Christians took this reference in Psalm 110 to deny that Jesus was of the lineage of the Levitical priests; instead, he was connected back to a mysterious king named Melchizedek in the time of Abraham (Genesis 14:17; Hebrews 7:1–9). They wanted to repudiate the Jewish priesthood and suggest Jesus came from a "heavenly" lineage (Hebrews 7:16). But that is obviously not the original meaning of this Psalm, attributed to King David. He is envisioning the ideal future Messiah or king, one of his descendants, as also priestly.

CHAPTER EIGHT: MARY IN JERUSALEM

114 But this Ephesus site: See Tom Bissell's entertaining account in *Apostle*, 212–255. Stephen J. Shoemaker has done the definitive work on Mary's last days in Jerusalem, see his comments on the alternative sites at Constantinople and Ephesus in *Ancient Traditions*, 71–76.

115 The John who lived in Asia: There are two Johns in early Christian history and they are often confused. First, is John the son of Zebedee, the

fisherman, along with his brother James, who was one of the twelve apostles. Then there is John the Elder—who apparently did end up living at Ephesus in Asia; see Eusebius, *Church History* 3.29.4–7, and Bauckham, *Jesus and the Eyewitnesses*, 358–411, 550–589. This second John is the likely author of the letters of 1, 2, and 3 John in the New Testament, see Brown, *The Epistles of John*, and Mason and Robinson, *Early Christian Reader*, 532–595.

115 There is, however, persuasive evidence: See Tabor, "Who Was the Mysterious 'Disciple Whom Jesus Loved'?," Taborblog, December 20, 2015, jamestabor.com.

117 There we read the following account: Jerome, *Adversus Vigilantium* 2, in Hennecke and Schneemelcher, *New Testament Apocrypha*, vol. 1, 178.

118 This dynastic succession: See Josephus, *Jewish Antiquities* 20.200–201, on the death of James; Eusebius, *Church History* 2.1.2–4, 2.23.4–7, quotes numerous early sources including Clement of Rome and Hegesippus from the second century.

118 When Hadrian became emperor: Eusebius, *Church History* 4.5.2–5.

118 In later sources: Galatians 1:18, 2:9–12; Acts 15:13–22, 21:17–26; Josephus, *Jewish Antiquities* 20.200–201; Gospel of Thomas 12; Eusebius, *Church History* 2.1.3–4; 2.23.4–7.

120 It was there, on Mount Zion: Paul refers to the "brothers of the Lord" as married, presumably including James (1 Corinthians 9:5).

120 This is the same house: See Pixner, "Church of the Apostles," as well as his chapter "Mary on Zion" in *Paths of the Messiah*, 398–407.

121 It is what lies underneath: My student David Christian Clausen has published much of this latest research in his book *The Upper Room*; see 127–167. For a summary of his findings, see his "Archaeological Views" and, more recently, his "Hunting for the Upper Room in Jerusalem," Bible History Daily, July 16, 2024, biblicalarchaeology.org.

121 Given what we have learned: See the photos and descriptions of what we have uncovered so far of this "priestly mansion," at Philippe Bohstrom, "Archaeologists Uncover Life of Luxury in 2,000-year-old Priestly Quarters of Jerusalem," *Haaretz*, July 12, 2016, haaretz.com, and Jason Weaver, "Digging into First Century Jerusalem's Rich and Famous," Popular Archaeology, December 1, 2013, popular-archaeology.com.

122 The roof was flat: This description is based on excavations of first-century homes in what is now the Jewish Quarter of Jerusalem, as well as our excavations of a similar house on the slopes of Mount Zion, yards away from the Cenacle, applied to what still remains of the original floor plan and courtyard of the medieval structure, as well as subterranean areas.

123 One of our earliest records: *Itinerarium* 16. For a full discussion of the fourth-century references see Pixner, "Church of the Apostles."

123 In the Byzantine period: For the most up-to-date and comprehensive

survey of the archaeological discoveries in this area of Mount Zion after the destruction of Jerusalem in AD 70, see Shimon Gibson, "Reconstructing the Byzantine Church of Hagia Sion," 63–101.

CHAPTER NINE: HOW MARY WAS LOST

127 The early Christian historian Eusebius: Eusebius, *Church History* 3.12.1. English quotations of Eusebius are from *Eusebius: The Ecclesiastical History*, ed. and trans. Kirsopp Lake and J. E. L. Oulton, Loeb Classical Library, 2 vols. (Cambridge: Harvard University Press, 1926/1932).

127 One pious writer praises: Luigi Gambero, *Mary and the Father of the Church*, 30.

127 Notably, of Ignatius's four scant references: Ignatius, *Ephesians* 7.2, 18.2; *Trallians* 9.1–2; *Smyrnaeans* 1.1.

132 Stephen Shoemaker's pioneering work: *Mary in Early Christian Faith*.

135 Epiphanius asks: Epiphanius, *Panarion* 78.14.5–16.5.

135 The first, and more obvious: See Sarah Pomeroy's controversial but classic *Goddesses, Whores, Wives, and Slaves*.

136 They remind the soul: For texts, translations, and other related materials see my "Understanding Hellenistic Dualism," Taborblog, January 6, 2022, jamestabor.com.

138 Since we don't know when Mary died: As I have mentioned previously, the horrible bloody account of the murder of James by the high priest Annas, son of the same Annas who demanded Jesus be crucified, is recounted by the church historian Eusebius, who quotes an earlier Jewish Christian writer of the mid–second century, Hegesippus. James was thrown off the southeast wall of the temple enclosure into the Kidron Valley below, and then stoned and beaten to death with clubs. His brother Simon was looking on (*Church History* 2.23.3–18).

138 One of our earliest sources: Epiphanius, *Panarion* 78.11.2–3.

138 If a child made it: See Cokayne, *Experiencing Old Age;* see also Batrinos, "The length of life."

139 The traditional Tomb of the Virgin: Shoemaker, *Ancient Traditions*, 98–107. See also Finegan, *The Archaeology of the New Testament*, 179–181.

139 Stephen Shoemaker has exhaustively researched: Shoemaker, *Ancient Traditions of the Virgin Mary's Dormition and Assumption*.

140 Both Roman Catholic and Eastern Orthodox Christianity: See Shoemaker, *Ancient Traditions*.

141 What the dogma affirms: *Munificentissimus Deus: Defining the Dogma of the Assumption* (November 1, 1950) 44, vatican.va.

141 Six of the ten ossuaries: See Tabor, "The Talpiot 'Jesus' Tomb," 247–266, and "The Tombs at Talpiot: Overview of 'The Jesus Discovery,'" The Bible and Interpretation, April 2013, bibleinterp.arizona.edu.

142 Recent geochemical soil tests: See Tabor and Jacobovici, *The Jesus Discovery*, for a detailed overview. More recent scientific research has continued to advance the links between these tombs and their possible connection to Mary and her family. See Tabor, "New Evidence on the James Ossuary and its Probable Connection to the Talpiot Tomb," Taborblog, December 7, 2019, and "The Controversial James Ossuary and the Talpiot Tomb," Taborblog, February 13, 2014, jamestabor.com.

More recently there are new results supporting the same conclusions; see Shimron et al., "The Geochemistry of Intrusive Sediment Sample," and Matheson et al., "Molecular Exploration."

There is also the earlier preliminary research by Rosenfeld, Feldman, and Krumbein, "On the Authenticity of the James Ossuary," as well as Isabel Kershner, "Findings Reignite Debate on Claim of Jesus' Bones," *New York Times*, April 4, 2015, A4.

143 Those moments in the tomb: For a summary of the evidence for the possible identification of this tomb with Mary and her family, see my article "The 'Jesus' Tomb Story: Does the Evidence Add Up?" Taborblog, February 14, 2016, jamestabor.com.

CHAPTER TEN: MARY'S MESSAGE, THEN AND NOW

145 "arranging all things": Inscriptiones Graecae XII.2, 518.

146 In one of our earliest: See my article "John the Baptist: More Than a Prophet," 513–23, in *Enemies and Friends of the State: Ancient Prophecy in Context*, edited by Christopher A. Rollston (Winona Lake, IN: Eisenbrauns, 2018), as well as the major study by James F. McGrath, *John of History, Baptist of Faith: The Quest for the Historical John the Baptist* (Grand Rapids, MI: Eerdmans, 2024).

150 "walked with the Lord": Gospel of Philip, Nag Hammadi Codex II, 3, lines 59:6–11.

150 Mary's life spans the heyday: Josephus, who lived through the latter part of this zenith of messianic hope and ferment, is our most direct and important witness. In his two major works, *Jewish War* and *Jewish Antiquities*, he mentions over a dozen of these "messiah" figures either by name or by title—besides John the Baptizer, Jesus, and James—beginning with Hezekiah, whom the young Herod defeated in 47 BC. Here is the full list of the figures that Josephus highlights: Hezekiah, defeated by Herod in 47 BC (*Jewish War* 1.204–205); Judas son of Hezekiah, 4 BC at the death of Herod (*Jewish War* 2.56); Simon of Perea, 4 BC at the death of Herod (*Jewish War* 2.57–59); Athronges the Shepherd King, 4 BC at the death of Herod (*Jewish War* 2.60–65); Judas the Galilean, AD 6 at the removal of Archelaus (*Jewish War* 2.118); Theudas, c. AD 44 (*Jewish Antiquities*

Notes

20.97); James and Simon, c. AD 46, sons of Judas the Galilean, crucified by Tiberius Alexander, nephew of Philo, who was procurator AD 46–48 (*Jewish Antiquities* 20.102); "the Egyptian," c. 50s AD (*Jewish Antiquities* 20.169–171; *Jewish War* 2.261–263; Acts 21:38); Eleazar son of Dineus, c. AD 52 under Felix (*Jewish War* 2.253; *Jewish Antiquities* 20.161); Menahem son of Judas the Galilean, AD 66 (*Jewish War* 2.433–448); Eleazar son of Jairus, commander at the fall of Masada in AD 73, of the family of Menahem (*Jewish War* 2.447).

151 As Hugh Schonfield put it: Schonfield, *The Lost "Book of the Nativity of John,"* 5.

153 Scholars have developed: Perrin, *Rediscovering the Teaching of Jesus.*

154 As a result of many decades: Although scholars seldom agree on every detail in isolating the "authentic" teachings of Jesus, a good guide is the marvelous little book by John Dominic Crossan, *The Essential Jesus.* Crossan has been the most influential scholar in this "quest" for the authentic sayings of Jesus.

155 The Torah and the prophets: Translations are mine: Mark 1:15; Luke 11:20 and 17:20–21; Mark 12:34; Luke 11:2 and 13:20–21; Mark 4:26–29 and 4:30–32; Luke 16:16.

156 Whoever would be great: Translations are mine: Luke 6:20–21; Matthew 5:3–11; Mark 10:28–31; Luke 12:22–30, 11:25, and 3:11; Matthew 5:42; Mark 10:42–4/Luke 22:25–26.

157 Do not swear: Translations are mine: Luke 6:14–15; Matthew 6:3, 5–7; *Didache* 1.6; Mark 2:15–17; Luke 6:31/Matthew 7:12; Matthew 23:25–26; Luke 6:45; Matthew 5:34–37.

157 Do not swear: Translations are mine: Matthew 21:31; Luke 14:21–24, 17:18; Mark 12:43–44; Luke 7:10, 10:38–42.

158 He even chooses a tax collector: Mark 2:13–17/Matthew 9:9; Mark 3:18.

158 In what is perhaps: Luke 10:29–37, 17:11–18; John 4:38.

159 He freely speaks with women: John 4:27; Mark 7:24–30.

160 Josephus says as much about: *Jewish Antiquities* 18.118.

161 If your brother or sister sins: Luke 6:27–29/Matthew 5:41; Matthew 26:52; Luke 6:35–36, 37–38; Luke 17:3; Mark 12:17.

162 In the Dead Sea Scrolls we read: 4Q 285, fr. 4 and 5.

162 As the scroll puts it: The War Scroll I, 5–7.

Bibliography

ANCIENT PRIMARY SOURCES

Epiphanius. *The Panarion*. Book I. Frank Williams, trans. 2nd ed., revised and expanded. Leiden, Netherlands: E. J. Brill, 2009.

Eusebius. *The Ecclesiastical History*. Edited and translated by Kirsopp Lake and J. E. L. Oulton. Loeb Classical Library, 2 vols. Cambridge, MA: Harvard University Press, 1926/1932.

Isenberg, Wesley W. "The Gospel of Philip." In The Nag Hammadi Library in English. Edited by James M. Robinson. San Francisco: Harper & Row, 1988.

Josephus. *The Life, Against Apion, The Jewish War,* and *Jewish Antiquities*. Edited and translated by Louis Feldman, Ralph Marcus, and H. St. J. Thackeray. Loeb Classical Library, 9 vols. Cambridge, MA: Harvard University Press. 1926–1963.

Inscriptiones Graecae, vol. XII, part 2: *Inscriptiones Lesbi, Nesi, Tenedi*. Edited by Ashley R. Paton. Berlin: G. Reimer, 1899.

The Apocryphal Old Testament. Edited by H. F. D. Sparkes. Oxford: Oxford University Press, 1984.

The Apostolic Fathers. Edited and translated by Bart Ehrman. Loeb Classical Library, 2 vols. Cambridge, MA: Harvard University Press, 2003.

The Complete Dead Sea Scrolls in English. 5th ed. Edited and translated by Geza Vermes. New York: Penguin Books, 1998.

The Holy Bible. Revised Standard Version. Oxford: Oxford University Press, 1952 and 1971.

The Old Testament Pseudepigrapha. Edited by James H. Charlesworth. 2 vols. Garden City, NY: Doubleday, 1983–85.

Bibliography

SECONDARY SOURCES

Adler, William. "Exodus 6:23 and the High Priest from the Tribe of Judah." *Journal of Theological Studies* 48, no. I (1997): 24–47.

———. "On the Priesthood of Jesus: A New Translation and Introduction." In *New Testament Apocrypha: More Noncanonical Scriptures*, vol. I, eds. Tony Burke and Brent Landau. Grand Rapids, MI: Eerdmans, 2016.

Alderman, Naomi. *The Liar's Gospel: A Novel*. New York: Back Bay Books/Little, Brown and Company, 2013.

Aptowitzer, Victor. *Parteipolitik der Hasmonäerzeit im rabbinischen und pseudoepigraphischen Schrifttum*. Wien: Verlag der Kohut-Foundation, 1927.

Athans, Mary C. *In Quest of the Jewish Mary: The Mother of Jesus in History, Theology, and Spirituality*. Maryknoll, NY: Orbis, 2013.

Barrett, J. Edward. "Can Scholars Take the Virgin Birth Seriously?" *Bible Review* 4, no. 5 (1988): 10–11, 13–15, 29.

Batrinos, Menelaos L. "The length of life and *eugeria* in classical Greece." In *Hormones (Athens, Greece)* 7, no. I (2008): 82–3.

Bauckham, Richard. *Jesus and the Eyewitnesses: The Gospels as Eyewitness Testimony*. 2nd ed. Grand Rapids, MI: Eerdmans, 2017.

———. *Jude and the Relatives of Jesus in the Early Church*. Edinburgh: T. & T. Clark, 1990.

———. "Salome the Sister of Jesus, Salome the Disciple of Jesus, and the Secret Gospel of Mark." *Novum Testamentum* 33, no. 3 (1991): 245–75. doi:10.2307/1561359.

———. "The Brothers and Sisters of Jesus: An Epiphanian Response to John P. Meir." *Catholic Biblical Quarterly* 56 (1994): 686–700.

———. "The Relatives of Jesus," *Themelios* 21, no. 2 (January 1966): 18–21.

Behar, Doron M., et al. "The Matrilineal Ancestry of Ashkenazi Jewry: Portrait of a Recent Founder Event." *American Journal of Human Genetics* 78, no. 3 (2006): 487–97.

Benko, Stephen. *The Virgin Goddess: Studies in the Pagan and Christian Roots of Mariology*. Leiden, Netherlands: E. J. Brill, 1993.

Bennema, Cornelis. "The Beloved Disciple: The Unique Eyewitness" and "The Mother of Jesus: A Catalyst in His Ministry." In *Encountering Jesus: Character Studies in the Gospel of John*. Minneapolis: Augsburg Fortress Press, 2014.

Billig, Yaʿakov, Liora Freud, and Efrat Bocher. "A Luxurious Royal Estate from the First Temple Period in Armon ha-Natziv, Jerusalem." *Tel Aviv* 49:1 (2022): 8–31.

Bissell, Tom. *Apostle: Travels Among the Tombs of the Twelve*. New York: Vintage, 2017.

Blinzler, Josef. *Die Brüder und Schwestern Jesu. SBS Journal* 21. Stuttgart: Katholisches Bibelwerk, 1967.

Boss, Sarah Jane, ed. *Mary: The Complete Resource*. New York: Oxford University Press, 2007.

Brock, Ann Graham. *Mary Magdalene, the First Apostle: The Struggle for Authority*. Harvard Theological Studies 51. Cambridge, MA: Harvard University Press, 2003.

Brown, Rachel Fulton. "The Quest for the Historical Mary," review of *Mary in Early Christian Faith and Devotion* by Stephen J. Shoemaker. *First Things*, June 2017.

Brown, Raymond. *The Birth of the Messiah: A Commentary on the Infancy Narratives in the Gospels of Matthew and Luke*. Anchor Yale Bible Reference Library. New Haven: Yale University Press, 1999.

———. *The Epistles of John*. Anchor Yale Bible Reference Library 30. Garden City, NY: Doubleday, 1982.

Brown, Raymond E., Karl P. Donfried, Joseph A Fitzmyer, and John Reumann, eds. *Mary in the New Testament: A Collaborative Assessment by Protestant and Roman Catholic Scholars*. Philadelphia: Fortress Press, 1978.

Brownlee, William H. "The Wicked Priest, the Man of Lies, and the Righteous Teacher: The Problem of Identity." *Jewish Quarterly Review* 73, no. 1 (1982): 1–37.

Buby, Bertrand. *Mary of Galilee*. Vol. 1, *Mary in the New Testament*; vol. 2, *Woman of Israel, Daughter of Zion*; vol. 3, *The Marian Heritage of the Early Church*. New York: Alba House, 1994–1997.

Burke, Tony, and Brent Landau, eds. *New Testament Apocrypha: More Noncanonical Scriptures*. Vol 1. Grand Rapids, MI: Eerdmans, 2016.

Bütz, Jeffery L. *The Brother of Jesus and the Lost Teachings of Christianity*. Rochester, VT: Inner Traditions, 2005.

Cartlidge, David R. " 'How Can This Be?' " *Bible Review* 18, no. 6 (2002): 28–31, 35–39, 60.

Casey, Maurice. *Jesus of Nazareth*. London: T&T Clark, 2010.

Čéplö, Slavomir. "The Life of John the Baptist by Serapion: A New Translation and Introduction." In *New Testament Apocrypha: More Noncanonical Scriptures*. Vol 1. Edited by Tony Burke and Brent Landau. Grand Rapids, MI: Eerdmans, 2016.

Charlesworth, James H. *The Beloved Disciple: Whose Witness Validates the Gospel of John*. Valley Forge, PA: Trinity Press International, 1995.

———. ed. *The Tomb of Jesus and His Family? Exploring Ancient Jewish Tombs Near Jerusalem's Walls*. Grand Rapids, MI: Eerdmans, 2013.

Chilton, Bruce. *Rabbi Jesus*. New York: Doubleday, 2000.

———, and Jacob Neusner. *James the Brother of Jesus: James the Just and His Mission*. Louisville, KY: Westminster John Knox Press, 2001.

Clausen, David Christian. *The Upper Room and the Tomb of David: The History, Art and Archaeology of the Cenacle on Mount Zion*. Jefferson, NC: McFarland & Co., 2016.

————. "Archaeological Views: Mount Zion's Upper Room and Tomb of David." *Biblical Archaeology Review* 43, no. 1 (2017): 24–25, 61.

Cohen, Shaye J. D. *From the Maccabees to the Mishnah.* Louisville, KY: Westminster John Knox Press, 1988.

————. *The Beginnings of Jewishness: Boundaries, Varieties, Uncertainties.* Berkeley: University of California Press, 2001.

Cokayne, Karen. *Experiencing Old Age in Ancient Rome.* Routledge Classical Monographs. London and New York: Routledge, 2003.

Condor, Major C. R. *Palestine.* 2nd ed. London: Philip & Son, 1891.

Cook, John Granger. "Crucifixion and Burial," *New Testament Studies* 57, no. 2 (2011): 193–213.

————. *Crucifixion in the Mediterranean World.* WUNT 327. Tübingen: Mohr Siebeck, 2014.

Crone, Patricia. "Jewish Christianity and the Qur'ān," Parts One and Two. *Journal of Near Eastern Studies* 74. no. 2 (2015): 225–253 and 75, no. 1 (2016): 1–21.

Crossan, John Dominic. *The Essential Jesus: Original Sayings and Earliest Images.* Edison, NJ: Castle Books, 1994.

————. *The Historical Jesus: The Life of a Mediterranean Jewish Peasant.* San Francisco: Harper & Row, 1991.

————, and Jonathan L. Reed. *Excavating Jesus: Beneath the Stones, Behind the Texts.* San Francisco: HarperSanFrancisco, 2001.

Crouch, James E. "How Early Christians Viewed the Birth of Jesus," *Bible Review* 7, no. 5 (1991): 34–38.

Dark, Kenneth R. "Early Roman-Period Nazareth and the Sisters of Nazareth Convent." *Antiquaries Journal* 92 (2012): 37–64.

————. "Has Jesus' Nazareth House Been Found?" *Biblical Archaeology Review* 41, no. 2 (March/April 2015): 54–63.

————. *Sepphoris-Nazareth Survey: A Preliminary Report on the First Season's Work in 2004.* London: The Late Antiquity Research Group, 2005.

Deissmann, Adolf. "Der Name Panthera." In *Orientalische Studien T. Nöldeke gewidmet.* Giessen: Brunnen Verlag, 1906.

————. *Light from the Ancient East: The New Testament Illustrated by Recently Discovered Texts of the Greco-Roman World.* Translated by Lionel R. M. Strachen from the 1922 revised 4th German edition. Grand Rapids, MI: Baker Book House, 1965.

Droge, Arthur J., and James D. Tabor. *A Noble Death: Suicide & Martyrdom Among Christians and Jews in Antiquity.* San Francisco: HarperSanFrancisco, 1992.

Ehrman, Bart. *How Jesus Became God: The Exaltation of a Jewish Preacher from Galilee.* New York: HarperOne, 2015.

————. *Lost Scriptures: Books That Did Not Make It into the New Testament.* New York: Oxford University Press, 2003.

————. *The New Testament: A Historical Introduction to Early Christian Writings.* 7th ed. New York: Oxford University Press, 2019.

Eisenman, Robert. *James the Brother of Jesus: The Key to Unlocking the Secrets of Early Christianity and the Dead Sea Scrolls.* New York: Penguin, 1997.

Elliot, J. K., ed. *The Apocryphal New Testament.* Oxford: Oxford University Press, 1993.

Evans, Craig A. "Death Becomes Him: On the Execution and Burial of Jesus," "'Hang Him on a Tree until Dead': Hanging and Crucifixion in Second Temple Israel," and "The Family Buried Together Stays Together: On the Burial of the Executed in Family Tombs." In *Jesus and the Remains of His Day: Studies in Jesus and the Evidence of Material Culture.* Peabody, MA: Hendrickson, 2016.

Feldman, L. H. "Josephus." In *The Anchor Bible Dictionary.* Edited by David Noel Freedman. New York: Doubleday, 1992.

————. *Josephus and Modern Scholarship, 1937–1980.* Berlin, New York: W. de Gruyter, 1984.

Feuillet, André. *Jesus and His Mother.* Still River, MA: St. Bede's, 1985.

Fiensy, David A., and James Riley Strange, eds. *Galilee in the Late Second Temple and Mishnaic Periods: The Archaeological Record from Cities, Towns, and Villages.* 2 vols. Minneapolis: Fortress Press, 2014, 2015.

Finegan, Jack. *Handbook of Biblical Chronology: Principles of Time Reckoning in the Ancient World and Problems of Chronology in the Bible.* 2nd ed. Peabody, MA: Hendrickson Publishers, 1998.

————. *The Archaeology of the New Testament.* Rev. ed. Princeton: Princeton University Press, 1992.

Fiorenza, Elizabeth Schüssler. *In Memory of Her: A Feminist Reconstruction of Christian Origins.* New York: Crossroads, 1994.

Folda, Jaroslav, "The Church of Saint Anne," *The Biblical Archaeologist* 54, no. 2 (1991): 88–96.

Foskett, Mary E. *A Virgin Conceived: Mary and Classical Representations of Virginity.* Bloomington and Indianapolis: Indiana University Press, 2002.

Fredriksen, Paula. *Jesus of Nazareth: King of the Jews.* New York: Vintage, 2000.

Funk, Robert, and Roy W. Hover. *The Five Gospels: What Did Jesus Really Say? The Search for the Authentic Words of Jesus.* New York: HarperOne, 1996.

Gambero, Luigi. *Mary and the Fathers of the Church: The Blessed Virgin Mary in Patristic Thought.* Translated by Thomas Buffer. San Francisco: Ignatius, 1999.

Gaventa, Beverly Roberts, ed. *Mary: Glimpses of the Mother of Jesus.* Columbia: University of South Carolina Press, 1995.

Gaventa, Beverly Roberts, and C. L. Rigby, eds. *Blessed One: Protestant Perspectives on Mary.* Louisville, KY: Westminster John Knox, 2002.

Geva, Hillel, et al., eds. Series published by the Israel Exploration Society in Jerusalem: *Ancient Jerusalem Revealed* (1976); *Ancient Jerusalem Revealed* (1994);

Bibliography

Ancient Jerusalem Revealed, Expanded Edition 2000 (2000); and *Ancient Jerusalem Revealed: Archaeological Discoveries 1998–2000* (2019).

Gibson, Shimon. *The Cave of John the Baptist: The Stunning Archaeological Discovery That Has Redefined Christian History.* New York: Doubleday, 2004.

———, and James D. Tabor. "John the Baptist's Cave: The Case For." *Biblical Archaeology Review* 31, no. 3 (2005): 37–41, 58.

———. "Reconstructing the Byzantine Church of Hagia Sion and the Crusader Church of Sancta Maria: New Insights from Archaeological Excavations Conducted on Mount Zion in the Nineteenth and Twentieth Centuries." In O. Peleg-Barkat, Yehiel Zelinger, Yuval Gadot, and Yiftah Shalev, eds., *New Studies in the Archaeology of Jerusalem and Its Region. Collected Papers.* Vol. XVII (2024).

Giordano, Frank R. Jr. "Chance and Choice in Thomas Hardy's 'Panthera.'" In *English Literature in Transition, 1880–1920* 14, no. 4 (1971): 249–256.

Gransden, Antonia. "The Growth of the Glastonbury Traditions and Legends in the Twelfth Century." *Journal of Ecclesiastical History* 27, no. 4 (1976): 337–58.

Gros Louis, Kenneth R. R. "Different Ways of Looking at the Birth of Jesus." *Bible Review* 1, no. 1 (1985): 32–40.

Hachlili, Rachel. *Jewish Funerary Customs, Practices, and Rites in the Second Temple Period.* Leiden, Netherlands: Brill, 2005.

Haupt, Peter, and Sabine Hornung. "Ein Mitglied der Heiligen Familie? Zur Rezeption eines römischen Soldatengrabsteines aus Bingerbrück, Kr. Mainz-Bingen." In memoriam James Whitehead. *Archäologische Informationen* 27.1 (2004): 133–140.

Hazleton, Lesley. *Mary: A Flesh-and-Blood Biography of the Virgin Mother.* New York: Bloomsbury, 2004.

Hennecke, Edgar, and Wilhelm Schneemelcher, eds. *New Testament Apocrypha.* Vols. 1 and 2. English translation edited by R. McL. Wilson. Rev. ed. Louisville, KY: Westminster John Knox Press, 1991, 1992.

Hock, Ronald F. *The Infancy Gospels of James and Thomas: With Introduction, Notes, and Original Text Featuring the NEW Scholars Version Translation.* Santa Rosa, CA: Polerbridge Press, 1995.

———, and David R. Cartlidge. "The Favored One." *Bible Review* 17, no. 3 (2001): 13–14, 16–18, 21–25.

Holzapfel, Richard Neitzel. "King Herod." *Brigham Young University Studies* 36, no. 3 (1996): 35–73.

Ilan, Tal. *Lexicon of Jewish Names in Late Antiquity, Part I: Palestine 330 BC–200 CE.* Texts and Studies in Ancient Judaism 91. Tübingen: Mohr Siebeck, 2002.

———. "'Man Born of Woman . . .' (Job 14:1): The Phenomenon of Men Bearing Metronymes at the Time of Jesus." *Novem Testamentum* 34, no. 1 (January 1992): 23–45.

Isbell, Charles D. "Does the Gospel of Matthew Proclaim Mary's Virginity?" *Biblical Archaeology Review* 3, no. 2 (1977): 18–19, 52.

James, M. R. ed., *The New Testament Apocrypha*. Oxford: Clarendon Press, 1924.

Johnson, Elizabeth A. *Truly Our Sister: A Theology of Mary in the Communion of the Saints*. New ed. New York/London: Continuum, 2009.

————. *Dangerous Memories: A Mosaic of Mary in Scripture*. New York/London: Continuum, 2004.

Jones, F. Stanley. *Which Mary? The Marys of Early Christian Tradition*. Society of Biblical Literature Symposium Series 19. Atlanta: Society of Biblical Literature, 2002.

Keynan, Eldad. "A Critical Examination of the Occurrences of Common Names, Rare Names, and Nicknames: The Name *Yose* (יוסה) from the Talpiot Tomb as a Test Case." In *The Tomb of Jesus and His Family: Exploring Ancient Jewish Tombs Near Jerusalem's Walls*. James H. Charlesworth, ed. Grand Rapids, MI: Eerdmans, 2013.

King, Karen L. *The Gospel of Mary of Magdala: Jesus and the First Woman Apostle*. Santa Rosa, CA: Polebridge Press, 2003.

Klausner, Joseph. *Jesus of Nazareth*. Translated by Herbert Danby. Boston: Beacon Press, 1964.

Krauss, Samuel. *Das Leben Jesu nach jüdischen Quellen*. 1902, rpt. Hildesheim: Olms, 2006.

Leith, Mary Joan Winn. "Earliest Depictions of the Virgin Mary," *Biblical Archaeology Review* 43, no. 2 (2017): 40–49, 68–70.

Levine, Amy-Jill, ed., with Maria Mayo Robbins. *A Feminist Companion to Mariology*. Cleveland: Pilgrim Press, 2005.

Levine, Amy-Jill, Dale Allison, and John Dominic Crossan, eds. *The Historical Jesus in Context*. Princeton: Princeton University Press, 2006.

Levine, L. I. "Herod the Great." In *Anchor Bible Dictionary*. Vol. 3. New York: Doubleday, 1992.

Lincoln, Andrew T. *Born of a Virgin? Reconceiving Jesus in the Bible, Tradition, and Theology*. Grand Rapids, MI: Eerdmans, 2013.

Mason, Steve, and Tom Robinson. *Early Christian Reader*. Atlanta: Society of Biblical Literature, 2013.

Matheson, C. D., K. K. Vernon, A. Lahti, R. Fratpietro, M. Spigelman, S. Gibson, et al. "Molecular Exploration of the First-Century *Tomb of the Shroud* in Akeldama, Jerusalem." In *PLoS One* 4:12 (2009): e8319. https://doi.org/10.1371/journal.pone.0008319

Maunder, Chris. "Mary in the New Testament and Apocrypha." In *Mary: The Complete Resource*. Edited by Sarah Jane Boss. New York: Oxford University Press, 2007.

McGrath, James F. *John of History, Baptist of Faith: The Quest for the Historical John the Baptist*. Grand Rapids, MI: Eerdmans, 2024.

————. "Was Jesus Illegitimate? The evidence of his social interactions." *Journal for the Study of the Historical Jesus* 5, no. I (2007): 81–100.

McKnight, Scot. "Calling Jesus *Mamzer.*" *Journal of the Study of the Historical Jesus* I, no. I (2003): 73–103.

————. *The Real Mary: Why Evangelical Christians Can Embrace the Mother of Jesus.* Brewster, MA: Paraclete Press, 2006.

Meier, John P. *A Marginal Jew: Rethinking the Historical Jesus.* Vol. I: The Roots of the Problem and the Person. New York: Doubleday, 1991.

————. "The Brothers and Sisters of Jesus in Ecumenical Perspective." *Catholic Biblical Quarterly* 54 (1992): 1–28.

Miller, Robert J. *Born Divine: The Births of Jesus and Other Sons of God.* Salem, OR: Polebridge Press, 2003.

Molnar, Michael R. *The Star of Bethlehem: The Legacy of the Magi.* New Brunswick, NJ: Rutgers University Press, 1999.

Mourad, Suleiman A. "Mary in the Qur'an: A Reexamination of Her Presentation." In *The Qur'an in Its Historical Context.* Edited by Gabriel Said Reynolds. London: Routledge, 2008.

Mulholland, M. Robert. "The Infancy Narratives in Matthew and Luke: Of History, Theology and Literature." *Biblical Archaeology Review* 7, no. 2 (1981): 46–50, 52–53, 56–59.

Murphy-O'Conner, Jerome. "The Cenacle—Topographical Setting for Acts 2:44–45." In *The Book of Acts in Its First Century Setting. Vol. 4: Palestinian Setting.* Edited by Richard Bauckham. Grand Rapids, MI: Eerdmans, 1995.

Netzer, Ehud, Rachel Bar-Nathan, Rachel Laureys-Chachy, Ya'akov Meshorer, and Silvia Rozenberg. *Hasmonean and Herodian Palaces at Jericho: Final Reports of the 1973–1987 Excavations.* Jerusalem: Israel Exploration Society, 2001.

Nitzsch, Karl Immanuel. "Über eine Reihe talmudischer und patristischer Täuschungen, welche sich an den mißverstandenen Spottnamen Ben-Pandira geknüpft." In *Theologische Studien und Kritiken* 13 (1840):115–20.

Nixon, Virginia. *Mary's Mother: Saint Anne in Late Medieval Europe.* University Park, PA: Pennsylvania State University, 2004.

Nordmann, Karl-Ulrich. "Pantera, der geheimnisvolle Vater Jesu und der Grabstein des Tiberius Julius Abdes Pantera." *Berichte zur Archäologie in Rheinhessen und Umgebung* 6 (2013): 61–72.

Oberlinner, L. *Historische Überlieferung und christologische Aussage: Zur Frage der "Brüder Jesu" in der Synopse.* Forschung zur Bibel 19. Stuttgart: Katholisches Bibelwerk, 1975.

Pagels, Elaine. *Miracles and Wonder: The Historical Mystery of Jesus.* Doubleday: New York, 1995.

Painter, John. *Just James: The Brother of Jesus in History and Tradition.* Columbia: University of South Carolina Press, 1997.

Patterson, L. "Origin of the Name Pantera." *Journal of Theological Studies* 19, no. 73 (October 1917): 79–80.

Pelikan, Jaroslav. *Mary through the Centuries: Her Place in the History of Culture.* New Haven: Yale University Press, 1996.

———, David Flusser, and Justin Lang, eds. *Mary: Images of the Mother of Jesus in Jewish and Christian Perspectives.* Philadelphia: Augsburg Fortress Press, 2005.

Perrin, Norman. *Rediscovering the Teaching of Jesus.* New York: Harper & Row, 1967.

Pitre, Brant James. *Jesus and the Jewish Roots of Mary: Unveiling the Mother of the Messiah.* New York: Image, 2018.

Pixner, Bargil. "Church of the Apostles Found on Mt. Zion." *Biblical Archaeology Review* 16 (May/June 1990): 16–17, 20–31, 34–35, 60.

———. *Paths of the Messiah and Sites of the Early Church from Galilee to Jerusalem: Jesus and Jewish Christianity in Light of Archaeological Discoveries.* Edited by Rainer Riesner. Translated by Keith Myrick, Sam Randall, and Miriam Randall. San Francisco: Ignatius Press, 2010.

———. "Mary in the House of David," "Mary on Zion," "The Kathisma Church (Mary's Repose) Rediscovered," and "The Nazoreans, Bethlehem and the Birth of Jesus." In *Paths of the Messiah: Jesus and Jewish Christianity in Light of Archaeological Discoveries.* Edited by Rainer Riesner. San Francisco: Ignatius Press, 2010.

Pomeroy, Sarah. *Goddesses, Whores, Wives, and Slaves: Women in Classical Antiquity.* New York: Schocken Books, 1995.

Reeves, John C. "The Meaning of 'Moreh Sedeq' in the Light of 11Q Torah." In *Études Qumrâniennes: Mémorial Jean Carmignac.* Edited by Émile Puech and Florentino García Martínez. Paris: Gabalda, 1988.

———. *Trajectories in Near Eastern Apocalyptic: A Postrabbinic Jewish Apocalypse Reader.* Resources for Biblical Study 45. Atlanta, GA: Society of Biblical Literature, 2005.

Richardson, Peter. *Herod: King of the Jews and Friend of the Romans.* Studies on Personalities of the New Testament. Columbia: University of South Carolina Press, 1996.

Robinson, James M. *The Nag Hammadi Library.* Rev. ed. New York: HarperOne, 1990.

Rollston, Christopher A., ed. *Enemies and Friends of the State: Ancient Prophecy in Context.* Winona Lake, IN: Eisenbrauns, 2018.

Rooke, W. Deborah. *Zadok's Heirs: The Roll and Development of the High Priesthood in Ancient Israel.* New York: Oxford University Press, 2000.

Rosenfeld, Amnon, Howard R. Feldman, and Wolfgang E. Krumbein. "On the Authenticity of the James Ossuary and Its Possible Link to the 'Jesus Family Tomb.'" In *The Tomb of Jesus and His Family? Exploring Ancient Jewish Tombs*

Near Jerusalem's Walls. Edited by James H. Charlesworth. Grand Rapids, MI: Eerdmans, 2013.

Rubin, Miri. *Mother of God: A History of the Virgin Mary.* New Haven: Yale University Press, 2010.

Samuelsson, Gunnar. *Crucifixion in Antiquity: An Inquiry into the Background and Significance of the New Testament Terminology of Crucifixion.* 2nd ed. WUNT II/310. Tübingen: Mohr Siebeck, 2013.

Sandmel, Samuel. "Herod." In *Interpreter's Dictionary of the Bible.* Nashville: Abingdon, 1962.

———. *Herod: Profile of a Tyrant.* Philadelphia: Lippincott, 1967.

Sawicki, Marianne. *Crossing Galilee. Architectures of Contact in the Occupied Land of Jesus.* Harrisburg, PA: Trinity Press International, 2000.

Saxby, Alan. *James, Brother of Jesus, and the Jerusalem Church: A Radical Exploration of Christian Origins.* Eugene, OR: Wipf & Stock, 2015.

Schaberg, Jane. "Before Mary: The Ancestresses of Jesus." *Bible Review* 20, no. 6 (2004): 13–18, 20–23.

———. *The Illegitimacy of Jesus: A Feminist Theological Interpretation of the Infancy Narratives.* Expanded Twentieth Anniversary Edition. Sheffield, UK: Sheffield Phoenix Press Ltd., 2006.

———. *The Resurrection of Mary Magdalene: Legends, Apocrypha, and the Christian Testament.* New York: Continuum, 2004.

Schaefer, Jame. *Advancing Mariology: The Theotokos Lectures, 2008-2017.* Marquette Studies in Theology 89. Milwaukee: Marquette University Press, 2017.

Schäfer, Peter. *Jesus in the Talmud.* Princeton: Princeton University Press, 2007.

Schoenfeld, Andrew J. "Sons of Israel in Caesar's Service: Jewish Soldiers in the Roman Military." *Shofar: An Interdisciplinary Journal of Jewish Studies* 24, no. 3 (2006): 115–126.

Schonfield, Hugh J. *According to the Hebrews: A New Translation of the Jewish Life of Jesus (the Toldoth Jeshu), with an Inquiry into the Nature of Its Sources and Special Relationship to the Lost Gospel According to the Hebrews.* London: Duckworth, 1937.

———. *The Lost "Book of the Nativity of John": A Study of the Messianic Folklore and Christian Origins with a New Solution to the Virgin-Birth Problem.* Edinburgh: T. & T. Clark, 1929.

Schweitzer, Albert. *The Quest of the Historical Jesus: A Critical Study of Its Progress from Reimarus to Wrede.* Translated by W. Montgomery. New York: Macmillan Company, 1955.

Shanks, Hershel. "Where Mary Rested." *Biblical Archaeology Review* 32, no. 6 (2006): 44, 46–51.

Shimron, Aryeh, et al. "The Geochemistry of Intrusive Sediment Sample from the 1st Century CE Inscribed Ossuaries of James and the Talpiot Tomb in Jerusalem." *Archaeological Discovery* 8 (2020): 92–115.

Shoemaker, Stephen. "A Case of Mistaken Identity?: Naming the 'Gnostic Mary.'" In *Which Mary? Marys in Early Christian Tradition*. Edited by F. Stanley Jones. SBL Symposium Series 19. Atlanta: Society of Biblical Literature, 2002.

———. *Ancient Traditions of the Virgin Mary's Dormition and Assumption*. Oxford Early Christian Studies. New York: Oxford University Press, 2002.

———. *Life of the Virgin: Maximus the Confessor*. New Haven: Yale University Press, 2016.

———. *Mary in Early Christian Faith and Devotion*. New Haven and London: Yale University Press, 2016.

———. "Rethinking the 'Gnostic Mary': Mary of Nazareth and Mary of Magdala in Early Christian Tradition." *Journal of Early Christian Studies* 9 (2001): 555–595.

———. "The Virgin Mary in the Ministry of Jesus and the Early Church According to the Earliest Life of the Virgin." *Harvard Theological Review* 98 (2005): 441–467.

Smith, Morton. *Clement of Alexandria and a Secret Gospel of Mark*. Cambridge, MA: Harvard University Press, 1973.

———. *Jesus the Magician*. San Francisco: Harper & Row, 1978.

Smith, Preserved. *A Short History of Christian Theophagy*. Chicago: Open Court, 1992.

Spong, John Shelby. *Born of a Woman: A Bishop Rethinks the Birth of Jesus*. San Francisco: HarperSanFrancisco, 1992.

Strange, James F. "Sepphoris." *Bible and Interpretation* (September 2001).

Syon, Danny. *Small Change in Hellenistic-Roman Galilee: The Evidence from Numismatic Site Finds as a Tool for Historical Reconstruction*. Numismatic Studies and Researches XI. Jerusalem: Israel Numismatic Society, 2015.

Tabor, James. *Paul and Jesus: How the Apostle Transformed Christianity*. New York: Simon & Schuster, 2012.

———. *Paul's Ascent to Paradise: The Apostolic Message and Mission of Paul in the Light of His Mystical Experiences*. Charlotte, NC: Genesis 2000 Publishing, 2020.

———. "Returning to the Divinity: Josephus's Portrayal of the Disappearances of Enoch, Elijah, and Moses." *Journal of Biblical Literature* 108 (1989): 225–38.

———. "Testing a Hypothesis." Forum on the Talpiot "Jesus" Family Tomb. In *Near Eastern Archaeology* 69, nos. 3–4 (2006): 132–136.

———. *The Jesus Dynasty: The Hidden History of Jesus, His Royal Family, and the Birth of Christianity*. New York: Simon & Schuster, 2006.

———. "The Talpiot 'Jesus' Tomb: A Historical Analysis." In *The Tomb of Jesus and His Family? Exploring Ancient Jewish Tombs Near Jerusalem's Walls*. Edited by James H. Charlesworth. Grand Rapids, MI: Eerdmans, 2013.

————. *Things Unutterable: Paul's Ascent to Paradise in its Greco-Roman, Judaic, and Early Christian Contexts.* Studies in Judaism. Lanham, MD: University Press of America, 1986.

————, and Simcha Jacobovici. *The Jesus Discovery: The New Archaeological Find That Reveals the Birth of Christianity.* New York: Simon & Schuster, 2012.

Talbert, Charles H. "Miraculous Conceptions and Births in Mediterranean Antiquity." In *The Historical Jesus in Context.* Edited by Amy-Jill Levine, Dale C. Allison, and John Dominic Crossan. Princeton: Princeton University Press, 2006.

Taylor, Joan E. *Boy Jesus: Growing Up Judean in Turbulent Times.* London: SPCK Publishing, 2025.

Tóibín, Colm. *The Testament of Mary: A Novel.* New York: Scribner, 2014.

Van Aarde, Andries. *Fatherless in Galilee: Jesus As Child of God.* Harrisburg, PA: Trinity Press International, 2001.

Wacholder, Ben Zion. "Chronomessianism: The Timing of Messianic Movements and the Calendar of Sabbatical Cycles." *Hebrew Union College Annual* 46 (1975): 201–218.

————. "The Calendar of Sabbatical Cycles During the Second Temple and the Early Rabbinic Period." *Hebrew Union College Annual* 44 (1973): 53–196.

Ward, Seth. "Sepphoris in Sacred Geography." In *Galilee through the Centuries: Confluence of Cultures.* Edited by Eric M. Meyers. Duke Judaic Studies Series 1. Winona Lake, IN: Eisenbrauns, 1999.

Wilson, Barrie. *How Jesus Became Christian.* New York: St. Martin's Press, 2008.

Wray, T. J. *Good Girls, Bad Girls of the New Testament: Their Enduring Lessons.* Lanham, MD: Rowman & Littlefield, 2016.

Zeichmann, Christopher B. "Jesus 'ben Pantera': An Epigraphic and Military Historical Note." *Journal for the Study of the Historical Jesus* 18 (2020):141–155.

Zivie, Alain. "Pharaoh's Man, 'Abdiel: The Vizier with a Semitic Name." *Biblical Archaeology Review* 44, no. 4 (2018): 22–31, 64–66.

Index

Index

Index

Index

Index

Index

Index

ILLUSTRATION CREDITS

Balage Balogh, artist, used with permission: 18, 38
Wikimedia Commons: 10, 25, 98, 140, 153, 161
Lori Woodall: 4, 27, 33, 40, 52, 53, 63, 66, 70, 105, 114, 119, 124, 128
Lori Woodall, Kröller-Müller Museum, Otterlo, Netherlands: 159
Lori Woodall, Kunsthalle, Hamburg: 57
Lori Woodall, National Gallery of Art: 84
Lori Woodall, original painting owned by James D. Tabor: 165
Lori Woodall, Prado, Madrid: 132
Lori Woodall, Römerhalle, Bad Kreuznach, Germany: 91
Lori Woodall, Staatliche Museen zu Berlin: 80

A NOTE ON THE TYPE

The text of this book was set in Centaur, the only typeface designed by Bruce Rogers (1870–1957), the well-known American book designer. A celebrated penman, Rogers based his design on the roman face cut by Nicolas Jenson in 1470 for his Eusebius. Jenson's roman surpassed all of its forerunners and even today, in modern recuttings, remains one of the most popular and attractive of all typefaces.

The italic used to accompany Centaur is Arrighi, designed by another American, Frederic Warde, and based on the chancery face used by Lodovico degli Arrighi in 1524.

Composed by North Market Street Graphics,
Lancaster, Pennsylvania

Designed by Michael Collica